# muttle

## by tobyn tolini

Tolini Publishing LLC

Published by Tolini Publishing, LLC

Copyright © 2014 by Tobyn Tolini
303 437 2473

ISBN-13: 978-1505406412
ISBN-10: 1505406412

Book Design by Cherished Solutions, llc.
www.cherishedsolutions.com

I have tried to recreate events, locales and conversations from my memories of them. In order to maintain their anonymity in some instances I have changed the names of individuals and places, I may have changed some identifying characteristics and details such as physical properties, occupations and places of residence.

Manufactured in the USA
First Published December, 2014

# Dedication

*This book is dedicated to the lost ones with mental illness.*

# Introduction

"**M**uttle" is a first- hand experience of mental illness for families, students and anyone who is interested in learning "how it feels".

This book is not about success or failure. This book is not about working your way to the top or being a savior or a monster. This book is not about telling someone what they want to hear. This book is about finding truth in a world of neon lights and screaming nightmares. This book is the autobiography of three years of my life and the footsteps that lead to those three years. This book is fiction because if it were nonfiction it would be the truth and in this story the truth is hard to define. This book is about survival -- my survival. Looking back is to take sand paper to the skin, but that is where I went. My past is like a wheel on fire. Could I push through the flames?

# Part I

**Before the Flood**

# 1

## Chapter One

There is nothing sweeter than stepping onto a boat and knowing it's an all day expedition. Leaving the dock you look back and see no land, which can make you a little uneasy, but it's also exciting to know that the boat you're on is a little island. The boat slips through the water. The ocean air has the faint smell of salt as the wind hits your face, while the boat itself smells like fish from all the fresh catches. As you look into the water you see nothing. It is dark and murky.

My family loved to fish and one time we caught 54. It was a stormy day and the waters were wild. The ride out on the turbulent ocean made my stomach turn. I remember the waves being so high that they looked like they would drown the boat. My cousin Danny and I stood in the bow. We watched the waves come in. The boat went up and down and it looked like at any moment the waves would engulf us. Danny and I were alone, two little boys watching. We stood in awe. The waves were relentless. Up and down. Up and down. Finally my mom grabbed us and pulled us into the cabin.

The rest of the ride was interesting, but the whole time I wanted to be back on the bow, watching the stormy ocean, being assaulted by the wind. The ocean was beautiful. I enjoyed that feeling, that roller coaster sensation when you're not sure you'll make it to the end.

That day I saw myself as an invincible force battling an unknown foe and I had more power and more weapons than any army in the world. I was fearless with no guilt or shame or regrets; that would come later. I could do anything and I could be anything, a savior or a monster. I felt it and I knew it.

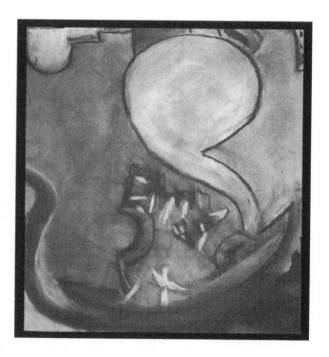

# 2

## Past and Pending

Life begins rather precariously and my beginning was no exception. My mom and my father couldn't have children and had adopted two children before I came along. It was something with my father. He had an infection when he was young and all his sperm were dead. The doctors told my parents their chance of having a child was a million to one. They won the lottery and I was conceived. I was the one in a million.

I was a passionate child and my main purpose in life was to have as much fun as possible. I would get up in the middle of the night just to ride my rocking horse. I would throw a baseball against a fence for hours. There's a video of me one Christmas when I was about four years old focusing on being Superman. Listening to the old Christopher Reeves Superman soundtrack with my Superman action figure held high. I was completely involved, being the one perfect superhero. I made the sound of swoosh and then zang while the music blasted. I walked from one end of the house to the other making Superman do whatever I wanted him to do, completely unaware of people around me. The melody and pulse of the music took me totally into the world of the "man of steel." I was unaware that my father was filming me.

There were always friends around my family back then. They loved my family. I was born into money and my parents were generous with it. My mom was always the woman who took in the children who needed a home; so not only did we have lots of friends around but we also had lots of extra kids around. They stayed for a while and then were gone. It wasn't foster care; it was just my mom being used by relatives or friends when they felt they needed a break. Once a cousin brought her one year old and two year old and left them with us for three months. Money and kindness buy friends; the same friends who leave when things get tough. When things get gristly and the money is all gone these so-called friends (and relatives) turn their back on you. They look at you and don't see you anymore. Those friends are gone now because the money is gone.

My father decided to create a franchise of Italian restaurants when I was in high school. He worked hard at getting investors and opened five restaurants. Eventually, they went bankrupt and so did my father. He lost everything.

Before the Italian restaurant adventure my father traveled internationally. He was like Santa Claus. He came home bearing gifts and mementos of his travels. He would walk in the door and yell my mom's name and then hug us all and ask, "What's for Dinner?" He was a successful salesman/entrepreneur when I was young and the telephone was his best friend and constant companion. He never sat and talked on the phone. He paced. Every phone in our home had a 20 foot cord and he used all 20 feet.

My father was loud, talked fast, and loved sports. No one in our home could utter or squeak a word when sports were on television. He planned his trips around the Broncos. My brother and I played soccer, football, baseball, basketball, and tennis. My father was always there coaching or yelling, and always pacing. He ached for us to be the best in sports. His expectations were great and he pulsed with the desire for us to always win.

He had season tickets to the Broncos and rarely missed a game. He generally took us with him. One of the most profound memories of my father was being lifted above the screaming fans when the Broncos made a touchdown. He wanted me to see above the crowd and genuinely cared for me to see. I loved him for that.

My father was also a clean freak. Our home was always spotless. He wanted it that way. He never walked by the kitchen sink without polishing the chrome and admonishing my mom for throwing the kitchen rag over the faucet.

My mom was an enabler. She could be talked into anything and would go the extra mile for any of us even when she knew our endeavors were hopeless. She laughed and sang but I also saw her cry. When she was pushed too hard she would scrub floors and cry. She always had crazy projects and seemed to think that everyone in the family should be as passionate about her projects as she. She talked about prophecy and the 'end of the world.' She wanted us all to be ready for that momentous event. She stored canned food and told us to come straight home if all the machines stopped working. Many nights I laid in my bed thinking about how I could possibly find my way home from school if all the machines stopped working. I know she didn't mean to scare us but we were scared by her prophecy talk. Maybe she was right and the machines will all stop working someday but that wasn't something that a child should have to ponder.

My brother was true. My whole life I looked up to him. He was my second hero. Superman was #1. My brother and I both liked the wrestling shows on television and he practiced on me. He is five years older than me so he could throw me around like a ragdoll. I tried to defend myself but he could always lift me above his head and slam me onto the ground. Just before I hit the floor he caught me and I don't remember ever being hurt. He definitely played an important role in my childhood by beating me at everything, which helped make me competitive, but taught me to be a good loser.

We moved from one big house to another about every two to three years. My father was always changing jobs. One job took the family to Florida. The year we moved to Florida my brother was a senior in high school. He stayed in Colorado for his senior year because of football and because he didn't want to miss out on the senior year fun with his friends. I missed him and was determined to shape myself into what I perceived he would want me to be. This, along with my father's desire for me to shine, pulled me into a frenzy of trying to be the greatest at everything I tried. With my brother gone I spent my time between the basketball hoop in the driveway and the swimming pool in our back yard. I shot baskets until my fingers bled and then continued shooting after taping my fingertips with Band-Aides. I was in a baseball league and was the best catcher in the league. I could throw out a runner from my knees.

My sister and I held onto each other that year. We talked late into the night almost every night and formed a bond that will always be with us. We both hated being abandoned by our father in Florida (we were lucky if he was home for 12 hours during the week and he spent all of his time sitting in the lanai with a morose, non-communicative demeanor). I had no idea what was wrong but now understand that this was a year-long low after a lifetime of mania. Now, I can identify my father as Bipolar but during my childhood it was just who he was. I now understand that he was sick.

One day, about a year after we moved to Florida, he marched into the house and told us that we were moving back to Colorado. He told my mom to handle it, gave her a power of attorney to sell the house and left. He "had to get started on the new opportunities that were presenting themselves in Colorado." My mom put the house on the market, sold it, called packers and movers and back to Colorado we went. The only thing I remember about that trip was that my mom couldn't talk. She had laryngitis so we, my sister and I, could do anything we wanted without being reprimanded.

# 3
## Meeting Expectations

**M**y father pushed me more than the average child should be pushed. He wanted me to play sports in high school. At one point he bought me 25 footballs and a huge net and told me the only way I would make it into the NFL was as a field goal kicker because I just wasn't brawny enough. He made me kick the ball every day for an hour. My resentment toward him grew stronger and stronger.

Starting high school was easy. I lived the stigmas and stereotypes and was the quarterback. I was the best at everything because that is what my father wanted. When I started my second year in high school, I had a year of new beginnings. I broke my hand during a fit of rage in the middle of summer. I was sixteen and was upset about a guy my sister was dating. She seemed attracted to guys who were callous and had no desire to bring anything good into the world. My hand punched through a fence and I remember looking at my friends and saying, "I just broke my hand." I looked down and could see it all busted up like broken bricks. This made it difficult for me to throw a ball. Were my quarterback days winding down? In fact, my whole body was busted up. I had broken my nose in three different places, broken my elbow, broken two ribs and a finger. I dislocated my jaw and dislocated my knee cap seven times. From age five to sixteen I had been through the ringer.

My nickname in football was 'Turtle Tolini' because I was so slow. I'd had three major surgeries on my knee and in a sprint I was in a dead heat with the heaviest guy on the team. I couldn't run fast but I could throw a ball further and with more accuracy than anyone else on the team.

I had the cast taken off my hand three weeks before the season started. I could barely hold on to the ball because of atrophy but I was number one and I was going to go out on the field and compete. My big brother and my father were in the stands. My brother was an all conference center, which said a lot considering we went to a school with a 600+ graduating class. It was late afternoon and the sun was just going down. The football field was grassy green and I could smell the pine trees that lined the field. The coach had laid the white chalk earlier in the day and it was fresh and undisturbed. All my buddies were going through the warm up routine and I was eager to take the field. I felt the weakness in my hand but just knew I would be able to overcome and be the quarterback I had been in the past.

It was time to show my stuff. My confidence was dead on. I stood behind the center and he snapped the ball. I had taken hundreds of snaps before but this time when the ball came back and hit my hand, fire shot up to my elbow and I fumbled the ball. The second snap came and I got a chance to take my four steps back to hit my target. (My hand was already swelling.) I went back and threw a pass that looked more like a pitch. The coaches knew me and my abilities so they gave me more chances. I took four more snaps -- all of which shot pain to my elbow and all of which fell on the ground. I fumbled four times in a row. I remember looking at my father. His head was down and he wasn't talking to the other parents. I gave it my all but it wasn't enough. Finally, the coach told me to go play wide receiver. 'Turtle Tolini' echoed in my head. Someone as slow as me being a wide receiver was a joke. This realization hit hard. The moment he said wide receiver was the moment I knew I would never play football again. I finished out the day and the next day I gave my pads to the coach. It was hard to quit because I was smart enough to know that I was giving up an easier life in high school because of breaks that teachers give football players (and we all know that the girls love the jocks). When my father's head went down I knew I would never live up to his expectations and I knew that every game would be a confirmation of my failure.

Life after football was interesting. It is amazing how a kid can be popular one day and then be dropped from the list the next. I had to change my priorities and my MO. In the past it had been important to me to please my father and now that I knew I couldn't, I developed contempt for his consumer lifestyle and resentment toward him was growing daily.

I started my own method of consuming: commercials, sitcoms, movies about adversity, video games, MTV, Beatles albums and many other lifestyle changes. I guess I was no better than my father but I was looking for a place to fit in. I was trying to find my place and set new priorities. It seemed the only time I ever found any peace was when I was consuming. I was trying to stay on top of a world that didn't know my name. I was in love with a girl who had been my best friend for two years and I had to watch her every day holding hands with a jock football player in the halls. She would always smile at me, but I was not with her and I just had to deal with it. High school was an ugly time in my life.

I kept consuming and absorbing; going out with new stoner friends, drinking alcohol, going to restaurants, driving like a bat out of hell because it was cool. My addiction to marijuana started when I was sixteen. Pot and I had a love-hate relationship. She would send me into a huge depression, but let me see past the horizon. Some people can smoke a little bud and be content with that. But, if I was going to do it, I was going to do it to the max. I developed the art of consuming; tacos, pizza, Pearl Jam, images of beautiful girls in bikinis and car commercials where the music shows pink moons.

It was then that I picked up a guitar for the first time.

I realized I needed something to make me look unique. It is amazing how hard you try to impress in high school. I was passionate about music and if it took music to make me unique - so be it. I asked my mom if she would buy me a guitar and she said, "Sure!" She could see my depression and would have done anything to make me happy and alive again. So, I was sixteen and I was picking up the guitar for the first time. I wanted to learn how to play and I wanted to find some independence from my family.

The day we bought the guitar, I sat in my room afternoon and night and wailed away. When you first start to play guitar, wailing away at it is all you do. My mom came downstairs and picked up the guitar. She played about six old 'sixties' folk songs. She had a great voice and I was utterly amazed. She sort of gave me a little hope. She asked me if I wanted to take lessons and I told her, "No." I didn't want to fail again. If I were taking lessons and couldn't get it, how would that look to my father? If I just 'messed around' with it and didn't get it, he wouldn't think a thing about it.

I started digging through my CD collection looking for the right song I could learn. I found the perfect one and I was going to learn it if it killed me. I was a typical consumer but this song was a gift. It was honest and not plastic. I thought that it would open the door to other music that is raw and real. I chose 'Castles Made of Sand' by Jimi Hendrix. I put the CD in my stereo and listened to it. *'A little*

*Indian brave who before he was ten played war games in the woods with his Indian friends.'*

The song touched me and gave me chills. This music was where I wanted to be. I wanted to be wrapped up around the notes. I searched and searched for some guitar tablature, which is an easier way to learn and I finally found it. Basically, I learned it one part at a time. I figured if you could play Hendrix you could play anything. A sixteen year old mind just works that way. As I got older I realized that there is always something new to learn. I bled, I sweat, I swore and I cried over that song; real blood, calloused fingers, sweat and real tears. I finally played it for my family and they seemed impressed.

The guitar helped me gain confidence late in high school. Even while I was struggling with it, I knew that I was doing this myself. No one could take credit for my dedication to my guitar. I was totally in control of how much I learned and how much I practiced. The guitar did nothing for my popularity but it gave me something to focus on and conquer.

# 4

## On the Tracks

College is supposed to be a time of discovery and it is for most people but it was a time of complete chaos for me. I was filled with anger at my father and drank and smoked to dull the pain he created with the shocking news of his infidelity and betrayal of what I considered sacred. He announced during my freshman year of college that he no longer loved my mom and was and had been unfaithful for the past ten years! He wanted to stay married to my mom but wanted to keep seeing his girlfriends. My mom was completely devastated. She had no clue that he was living this double life. She divorced him and learned to live her own life. My father's announcement affected all of us but we had to find a way to move on.

My way: I smoked pot. It helped. This was also an unspoken bond that connected people. I also had parties every week my sophomore year of college. I lived off campus with my friends Caleb, Andrea and Shelly. Caleb was my ultimate true-blue friend. He and I would usually get the keg at around 12 o'clock with our fake IDs. We would put the keg on our back patio where cement turned into grass. Our house was gated and our parties rarely got broken up.

We would tap the keg early and soon the cards would come out and we would play poker for drinks. Caleb could drink. He could drink like no one I have ever seen. I could keep up with him to a point but I was always drunk before him. By nine o'clock everyone would show up and they were always welcomed by two cute sober girls (our roommates) and two wasted buffoons.

I kept tasting chocolate chip ice cream, commercials about surfing, commercials about skiing, hair spray, body spray, Chinese rugs, new carpet, new house, guys drinking beers, clubs, newlyweds, Mexico, Florida, cures for cancer, causes for cancer, causes for the environment, billboards of attractive people, tattoos, Monte Cristo sandwiches. I guess I am a byproduct of an over-stimulated generation, where success is your fad whether you are watching football with the guys, smoking dope with druggies or smoking dope with football guys. Society demands that we stay normal but we have to be unique. *So, can a man be normal and be unique?*

It all finally caught up to me when I flunked out my third year.

To celebrate flunking out of college, I took a trip to Europe. I backpacked and went to Ireland, England, France, Germany, Spain, Austria, Holland, Italy and Switzerland. I rode the trains from country to country and slept in the railcars. I couldn't help thinking of the bums who rode the trains during the depression just to keep moving. Sometimes there wasn't an open railcar so I had to shuffle my feet into someone's car. My guitar was my constant companion and sitting on the train I was able to nurture my poetic nature and my desire to be independent and invisible. No one was there to influence me or praise me or throw stones at me. I wrote songs and sang to myself while looking out the windows of the train or sitting on the steps of the hostels.

Sometimes when people would try to get into my railcar I would bring out my guitar and play horrible and scream so they would leave.

The views from the train were glossy pictures of starry nights like something from Van Gogh's pallet. The vineyards in Italy spoke to me of a quiet life, simple but complex. I found myself dreaming of having my own vineyard and living life making wine. It gave me a peaceful hue which saturated my soul.

In the countries I visited I found myself in cafés, drinking wine and reading. I found myself being a typical tourist finding all the hot spots and getting pure joy out of my discoveries. Museums were my favorite spots. I spent two days at the Louvre in Paris just walking and looking. However, at times I felt alone and wanted a greater connection.

In Switzerland I found friends to travel with. I was sitting on a back patio of a bar in Interlaken, Switzerland, playing my guitar when a tall slender blonde guy came up and asked me if he could play. I handed it over to him and he started playing some Grateful Dead. He was intense, passionate and serious. After playing he introduced himself as Jay. We sat on the patio amid the vines and flowers and talked about all the different music we loved. The day was winding down and Jay asked me if I wanted to go with him and his friend Eric to their dive bar. I tagged along expecting these guys to take me to another average smelly, dirty bar and was not disappointed. Their bar was like every other bar. There was nothing special about it but it was their bar. Jay bought a bag of weed and after the short walk back to the hostel we lit up.

Jay, Eric and I stayed in Interlaken for four days. The mountains reminded me of my home in Colorado. Because of the weed I had become quite melancholic. We decided to go to Germany. Jay had weed left and we didn't want to travel with it so I rolled a huge joint that we smoked on the walk to the train station. The walk, and the company I was keeping was nice. We passed the giant joint back and forth talking about the places we had been, and the places we wanted to go. When we arrived at the train station that would take us to Germany we got split up. While looking at the travel board I felt a pull on my backpack and Jay, in an urgent, paranoid voice said, "We have to go, and we have to hurry." We were running with giant backpacks and my guitar, laughing at how ridiculous we must look to the other travelers. We found the train and continued laughing until we landed in Germany.

Germany was fun. We found ourselves a treasure of a bar. The tavern was huge and it had long benches. The beers we drank were in huge steins and there was a band playing John Denver covers and German music. The band was so good you couldn't help dancing and so we danced, like free spirits with no eyes cursing us. Every night we went to the same bar because of the air that reflected joy.

After a few days in Germany we decided to go to Amsterdam for Queen's day. Queen's day in Amsterdam is like Mardi Gras. As the train pulled into Amsterdam we were excited but worried about finding a hostel. The streets were full of thousands of people. We found a hostel and the first thing we did after we got settled was find a coffee shop and smoke some ridiculously good weed. Walking down the street was a battle. There were drugged people everywhere and every one of them was in a world of their own. Each store had techno music blaring and as I walked I could hear two sounds from two places meeting with an off-kilter sound of music. Jay, Eric and I decided to go back to the hostel where the crowds wouldn't bother us. There was a back patio at the hostel and we sat looking at the stream below. The building across the street was tilted and reflected how the years had bent it. There was a cat on the window sill and it looked like he was going to fall into the stream. We were all waiting for the cat to do something but he found his way home in a window sill next to the one he was sitting on. This back patio was a nice place to unwind, have a smoke and shed the dregs of Europe from my mind.

The trip was over for me and it was time to go home. I had fun being by myself and finding a voice. I had many thoughts about coming home while I was in Europe, but I knew that I had to finish college. I had to be successful in the eyes of the world.

I accomplished my goal and finished college. My old friend Caleb and I took the same classes and our friendship flourished. I had a part time job during college in the casino town of Blackhawk. I bartended, made good money, and was able to live the way I wanted. There were great times with my school work, guitar, friends and family occupying my time. I liked bartending but only did it for about a year. It bothered me a great deal to watch people sit for hours on end, gambling their entire paycheck and leave the casino with a stricken look. It felt as though I had a part in their failure.

School was fun, but as a graduate I realized that I needed to find a place to fit in. My thoughts and dreams were vivid and real. I was alive and excited about colors and words and music and theories and ideas and food and touching and being touched. I was becoming more alive every day. I didn't know that my saga was just beginning. My brain was beginning to scramble and all it needed to put me over the edge was a trigger.

# 5

## A Night of Fallen Glass

June 2003 (One month after college graduation)

Another day at the coffee shop. I had quit my job as a bartender and found a new job. The coffee shop had just opened and it was squeaky clean. You have to love these new express lines that the world keeps creating. The corporate world is a silly stage, but working the express line seemed the only option for a college graduate who was looking for his place in the world. It seems trite to knock corporations. It has been done. There are so many people that speak the words of abuse of power and still bask in the glow of their consumption. But they don't do shit about it. I am one of those. My hypocrisy was thick. There are movies, statistics, and literature that talk of the non stop horror of capitalism and the 'westward expansion' of the world where the kings rule with scepters of consumer power and with the deception of lies.

The truth is I might have been happier digging ditches, but I had a degree in marketing and was peddling the next great addiction. The drug that makes people awake when they stayed up all night worrying about bills and watching eternal commercials on television about the latest gadget that they just can't live without. I saw those people every day and for some reason I loved to make them smile.

The coffee shop was slow because it was new, so it was a good excuse to stand around with fellow employees and weave webs. The city of Golden, where I lived, had its own pulse. There was just something about it that spoke calm. In the calm, my past and my dreams were hidden; tucked away in heavy mountains with tiny rocks to bounce ideas off.

The coffee shop didn't feel like work. It felt like a community.

When Zane, the shift supervisor, came in after my shift had started, I asked him if he wanted me to mop floors and he told me to wait until later. He said for us to just sit around and look busy. He was a great guy to work for and was as laid back and shiftless as the employees who worked under him. I jokingly told him that I would just keep wiping the one spot that I had been wiping when he came in and he told me that he didn't give a damn what I did.

I liked Zane. He had a good heart even though he lived in a world where people looked down on him because he was gay. Zane was bound to his friends because they accepted him as he was. He had his ears pierced with the gages set high. He also had tattoos of the American Red Cross on his forearms. I can't remember what they were supposed to mean.

Our friend Clair was in the back doing dishes, she was definitely the one who had the most intensity about work this night. She was a tall black girl with short blond hair. She liked to wear wigs and she looked good. She always looked good. She had style. No one could touch the confidence that swirled around her and dripped from her shoes. Some girls walk with their head up and some girls slouch. She always had her head up.

After sitting around doing nothing, Zane asked me if I would like to do some ecstasy with him. I half heartedly said I would and he told me he would arrange it. This idea of ecstasy grew in my mind all evening and by the time we got through rush and had the store wrapped for the night I was excited. I had done it before and it was fun. Whenever I thought about ecstasy, the thirty minute documentary on MTV popped in my head and I could see 'the before' and 'the after' x-rays of an ecstasy-girl's brain. It was disturbing, but I knew it was just a scare tactic of the "establishment." The brain scan showed huge pits. I knew the science behind it and basically ecstasy just releases serotonin which makes you overjoyed for four hours. I hated the way it made me feel and I loved the way it made me feel. You can tell it's not a natural drug like marijuana. The chemicals make you feel a hint of unnatural control. It felt to me like there was a layer of dirt covering me from one end to the other when in reality I knew that I was squeaky clean.

I lived in the middle of Golden with my friend Kelly. He was never home because he was always at his girlfriend's house. Kelly worked at another coffee house and he and I had been friends for three years. He was another of my good friends. Kelly was slender because he was a crazy mountain biker. He was constantly on his bike and competed nationally. Kelly and I bonded because we listened to the same music. When Kelly started spending all his time with his girlfriend I missed him, but, hey, he had to do what he had to do and it was okay with me. I pretty much lived alone.

Kelly and I had a humble apartment. Our back yard was a park. There was a tree in the middle of the park that was about ten feet around and all the lower limbs had been cut off. It was like one of those monster northern California trees because it was big and it was stately standing there all alone in the middle. The other trees in the park seemed to be worshiping that tree. The park also had a long bridge that stretched over Clear Creek. Clear Creek wasn't a stream and it wasn't a river. It was somewhere in between. It wasn't polluted and there were kayakers in it all the time. If you looked about a hundred yards down from the bridge you could see the water running into the Coors brewery. We lived right next to Coors and during specific times you could smell the hops.

That little park was a great place to sit and listen to music on my headphones. I loved Golden. It was part of a big city (Denver) with small town pulse to it. The meeting place in Golden was the Blue Canyon. It had an open mic night every week. I played if I wasn't working. It was always an interesting atmosphere. The people usually didn't listen to you, which was good and bad. It was good because it made it easier to play and sing with no one listening, but it was bad because no one was listening.

The next day slipped itself in like a secret lover sneaks into the bed of an unsuspecting but surprisingly happy recipient. I had to work again but before I went in I decided I would play guitar. I played and sang loud. I guess I liked the idea of someone in the apartment next door listening and saying, "Man, he is okay." I was way too insecure about my music.

After playing, I walked to the coffee shop and was greeted with smiling faces; not from customers, but from fellow employees. Zane was there and he started telling me about the party he went to the night before. He bragged about doing his 'poi' (poi is spinning fire). He took a rope and lit both ends and then threw it around making circles of fire.) He told me that he had contacted Alex and had gotten some ecstasy for us and we agreed to do it after work. Alex worked with us and was experienced at knocking heads with ecstasy.

Work was long. When you get yourself excited to do a drug it's hard to wait.

The shop closed, and it was time.

We pulled into Zane's apartment complex and Alex

was waiting. He was an interesting fellow. He had blond curly hair. We would talk about everything: relationships, religion, politics and whatever spilled out of our mouths. I liked the kid. He was part Italian, like me, which gave us a connection. (There is a rumor in my family about ancestors. My aunt has this creepy picture of a Native American woman. The picture is scary. As a child my cousin and I used to go in the closet where the picture was kept to see who could sit and look at it the longest. I always won. My mom said that on her side of the family there is some Native American blood. It might be true or it could just be family banter.)

The night had arrived and I was like a child outside a candy store. I was ready.

Zane offhandedly informed me that Claire was joining us which set me back on my heels. Claire had never done ecstasy and I was always nervous about someone doing it for the first time. It had different effects on different people. Some people do it and want to talk and chill. Others have sex. I'm the chill kind. Alex didn't care how many joined us and was happy to spread the joy.

We waited for Claire patiently. Zane lived with Lisa, a fellow employee. Lisa was a lesbian, which did not define her. She and Zane had lived together for about a year and they were good friends. My relationship with Lisa was awesome. She and I were truly simpatico. She had the earthy thing going on like me but our friendship was more than just that. She and I were connected by the knowledge that we could trust one another. It was just something that we had.

Lisa was in no mood to try mind altering drugs and that was cool with me. I never push that kind of thing on people. She was sitting on the floor and looked up at me. "Toby, how are you doing?"

I sat down next to her and said, "I will be doing much better in an hour."

She just laughed.

Claire finally knocked on the door. Zane and I ran

into the kitchen. We couldn't wait another minute. Out came the pills. They always looked so small.

We were in the kitchen and it was time. Claire only got one half because she had never done it before. Alex, Zane and I took one for now and one for later. It always takes a little while before it kicks in. The wait was fun.

As the hour went by we made our way into the trees. There were trails behind Zane and Lisa's apartment. It was fun walking through it waiting for the drug to kick in. We walked to a short bridge and finally it hit. Claire started talking. This isn't unusual. She kept talking and talking and talking. We set up camp at a place in the woods that was close to light and Claire was still talking. It was as though she had just been born and she couldn't help but describe everything she was thinking. We all started laughing. I have to be honest, I was attracted to Claire but I wasn't going to make a move. I knew that she was vulnerable because she just got out of a bad relationship and even though she was such an amazing woman I would never take advantage of her in this scenario. She and I were just good friends. The night had just begun and the conversations were open. We covered everything, all the basics. We were huddled and touching started. Touching on ecstasy is an experience. It feels good so it is not strange to jump over conventional boundaries.

Do you suppose there is a place on some strange planet where we could all be so close and open all the time? The night had a glow to it!

I eventually got my headphones and started listening to music and dancing. I couldn't stop myself. The band I was listening to was good. My friends were accustomed to me being obsessed with music so it was no surprise to see me jumping up and down like I was the lead dancer of a tribal war dance. I couldn't control myself and I didn't want to. The ground was beating on my feet. I looked over at Claire and she was laughing. She could see that I was free. She told me that I was cute.

I jumped back into the circle and we started talking again. Claire's head was in my lap. I started touching her hair because it felt so different from mine. I loved the way it felt and I couldn't stop touching it. We started talking about fathers.

"My father was never around."

"Me too! He left my family to go to Haiti and was consumed by Voodoo."

"Really?"

"No, Toby, you don't understand. It's his life. He's a good man but lives a twisted life."

"I didn't know it was an actual religion. That is crazy. My father is sort of the same. He tries so hard and always chooses the wrong path."

"Well, we have to move on."

"Definitely!"

It was time to dance some more. The energy was sharp. The main reason I wanted to dance was because Zane brought out his poi and starting spinning fire in amazing circles. I could visualize a giant fire bellowing. I was dancing and could feel something that I had never felt. I let it enter me. I praised the fire and something dark bellowed inside. In the tinsel glow I could see. I threw my beliefs to the side and followed into a madness. I accepted it. I could see it in the night, the darkness that covers the earth and the small little lights that ignited fire in my heart.

I stopped and felt the presence of something darker than coal.

"Fuck, what have I done? I've let something in."

The night sky broke out like shards of glass touching me. I'd let something in.

I walked over to the trees where my friends couldn't see me and I knelt down. My face was close to the dirt and I whispered that I was sorry. I was scared that He would not forgive me. He could see the evil I'd invited into my heart.

Rejoining my friends, the night of dancing and

smoking and talking and laughing and touching wound down. We moved the party to the apartments and woke Lisa. The darkness I felt melted away like ice cubes in the sun. I was me again. I was whole.

Lisa had a guitar in her hands. I looked at her and smiled. She always knew. She handed me the guitar. My friends were talking and I started playing. Suddenly a song was springing out of my mind and my fingers found the chords. Everyone turned toward me and they became silent. I had finally written a song that made people stop and listen! Alex told me how good it was and said I needed to write it down. He ran into the house and got a pad and paper. He handed it to me and I wrote the song down. I sat against a tree and felt rooted to the ground. I eventually stopped singing and everyone melted away into the night. We had our ecstasy night and now it was over. Or so I thought.

# 6

## The Afterglow

I slept until sunset the next day. I woke with a desire to meet the sunset. I walked through the park. I put my headphones on. I listened to a stand up baseline that rolled around like a blotted fury. I was calm and kept my eyes on a red sky. I headed to the coffee shop.

The afterglow is the day after ecstasy. Some people hate it and some love it. It is dark melancholy, but the lights are still bright. I always loved to be manic or depressed. I made it to the coffee shop and was welcomed by a regular customer. His name was Dan and he was always showing people their charts and telling them about their life. He believed he was Pete Coors's father in a past life. He also believed that in the beginning of his life he saw Satan. The Pete Coors thing was funny, but seeing Satan when he was a baby was the most ridiculous thing I had ever heard. He said that Satan had huge scales all over him. Dan wasn't right in the head. He claimed that his parents were both doctors in a psych ward and he had lived with mental patients his whole life. This was probably the only thing I believed about him. He was a swine and always had that accumulated white stuff on the corner of his mouth. He would spit when he was talking. He would twist things around when I spoke to him and it could get frustrating. I was friendly to him but he irritated me. I listened to his vomit of the mouth. He had read everyone's chart in the store, including mine, and had some interesting things to say about me. He told me that I had done a horrible thing in my past life but had also done great things. I lived in America during the Age of Aquarius.

The idea of reincarnation stuck with me. So many people. So many spirits. It made sense that life was a continuous thing that moved forward after death.

Conversation with Dan was boring and I wanted to be outside.

I walked up to the bar to get my coffee and Julie greeted me. She commented about Dan and how he had read her chart. She told me it was a little strange because he kept staring into her eyes. I just shook my head and smiled.

Julie and I had a good relationship. We talked about religion and movies. Her favorite movie was the 'Lord of the Rings' series. She knew I had Christian beliefs and I was probably the only Christian that she would call a friend. She was Wiccan and believed in a goddess (mother-nature) who controlled the growth of the earth. I liked her and I think the reason we could talk about spirituality was because of mutual respect and acknowledgement of our differences.

I needed to get out of there. Dan was looking my way again and I just didn't want to listen to him. On my way out I saw Alex and Lisa sharing a smoke. I joined them and had to bum a cigarette from Lisa. She gave me the business about how I had quit only to start again, but she smiled and gave me one.

The walk home was inspiring. It took me about ten minutes to get to my apartment and then leave again. I couldn't be confined. I had to be free to roam.

The sky was losing its red and becoming blue against Lookout Mountain. I felt somewhat elated with the base line pulsing in my head so I danced with the plush red, blue sky. I didn't care if anyone looked at me. The dance was sweet and calmly smooth.

I returned to my apartment. The afterglow was wearing off and the depression was setting in. I knew I was coming down so I rented a relaxing uplifting cheesy video where the guy gets the girl after facing his fears and overcoming some giant adversity. Halfway through the movie as I gazed into the television set something hit me. My brain was clicking and I couldn't concentrate on the movie. It started slowly but kept getting stronger. I tried to ignore it and ignoring it worked at first but it kept clicking and panic took me. My hands were clammy. *Click – Pause - Click - Pause.* There wasn't a solid rhythm to it which made it more frustrating. When the movie ended I forced myself into my bedroom and put my head on the pillow. *Click – Pause - Click - Pause.* I couldn't go to sleep so I grabbed my guitar. I put my guitar down and put my head back on the pillow to try to get past this weird trip. *It's got to be some weird side effect and my mind will get over it tomorrow.* My eyes closed.

The next day was difficult. I had to go into work

early and I was trying get over this crazy shit in my head. I did a good job of lying low and just working the bar. I still had the clicking in my head. I was working a six hour shift and by the time I got out I was crazed. I had driven to work, which was ridiculous because work was only two blocks away, but the car seemed comfortable. I had a Jeep. It was brand new one, which was a huge stress reliever because my last car was such a headache. My father went with me to buy it. My economics teachers always said to never buy a new car because it depreciated the second it left the lot. Oh well.

I was paranoid and there was a hopeless feeling that the paranoia would never stop. Days passed and I had to do something about the clicking, but I didn't know what, so I drove over to my mom's house. My sister and my little niece, Jayde, lived with my mom. I spent a lot of time there because of Jayde. She didn't have a solid male figure in her life because her dad divorced my sister when she was four months pregnant. They lived about ten minutes away so it was no big deal. As I walked through the door I saw a sweet kid who greeted me with, "Hello, Uncle Booie!" and wrapped her little arms around my leg.

No one knew about the clicking but I had to tell someone. I needed to know it would be okay. I could always talk to my mom even when things were rough. She was more than a mom; she was a friend, which is a rare thing. The fear and anxiety of the click - pause – click was not going away and it was scaring the shit out of me. I walked into the computer room where my mom was playing some Tetras-like game on the computer. I walked over and stood looking down at her.

My mom smiled. She turned off her game and said, "Hey Booie," (They all called me Booie. When she was a baby my niece nicknamed me because she couldn't say Toby.) "How is it going?"

My mom always had answers. Maybe she would be able to help. "Not good, Mom."

A frown flickered on her face and she asked, "What's going on, Toby?"

The clicking was just too much. I had to tell SOMEONE!

I spoke softly and said, "Mom, I have to tell you something and you won't be happy." (My mom knew about all the drugs I used to do.) "Mom, I did some ecstasy and my brain is freaking out."

"Oh, Toby." My mom was the kind of old-fashioned woman that had never done drugs of any kind. She had never even tried marijuana. My mom wouldn't even know what pot looked or smelled like.

I felt like I had disappointed her but I needed help. I said, "I don't know what to do. I poisoned myself and there is this weird clicking in my head. I am so freaked out. It's like I'm someone else."

My mom, the eternal optimist said, "What does it feel like? Are you sure it's the drug or could it be that you are just tired, or... maybe something else?"

I told her, "It feels like I have this pause in my head and I can see the pause and then there is a click."

Mom could see the anxiety oozing out of me and said, "Settle down, Toby, and just relax. I am sure it will go away. It's just temporary. Just don't worry. It will go away."

She didn't get it. She was just not getting it. I was almost in a panic and no one cared about this clicking in my brain. "I am trying to settle down. I'm just so afraid that it will never go away."

My sister heard the entire exchange between my mom and me and was angry with me. She said, "Toby, you're how old? What are you doing taking ecstasy? You should know better than to fool around with drugs."

I felt panic.

She dismissed my discomfort and as she walked out of the room. She said, "Just play a video game on the computer and relax."

I started playing a game and it did relax me. I was a big fan of computer games. I could see the clicking on the screen and it filled the pause and the clicking in my brain.

I stayed for dinner and played with Jayde but kept going back to the computer. The click – pause was under control when I concentrated on the game.

About a week passed and the clicking gradually stopped. It was a long week but I got through it. I felt like I would be able to go back to my old life but with a new outlook and with a will to not mess with any more drugs. I had learned my lesson.

A week passed and my father picked me up at my house to go to the hospital because my sister had an anaphylactic reaction to seafood. When anyone in my family is in trouble, our family responds and I had been called to the hospital by my mom.

Driving with my father brought to mind all the memories of the old sports days when he was my coach and I just wasn't performing up to par. My father asked a question that chased my memories away. I tried to refocus on my sister's crisis in the hospital and I continued to listen to him as we drove along.

He frowned and asked, "So, have you learned your lesson with drugs, Toby?" If he had any idea about the way I had lived the last few weeks he wouldn't have asked a question like that. He would have realized that I had learned my lesson. I wondered who had told him about my ecstasy experience.

I replied, "Sure." Maybe he was trying to help me. It just showed how clueless he was about my life.

He continued to frown and asked, "Are you still having the same issues you were having the other night when your mom called me?" (So Mom told him!)

"NO!" I responded with a shake of my head.

Now he was on a roll. He thought he had found a button he could push. "Have you found a job yet? You have a marketing degree, you know."

I again shook my head and softly said, "I'm working at the coffee shop." How did he think it made me feel to ask that kind of question when he knew that I was supporting myself doing what I wanted.

He started getting condescending. "Can't you find something that pays a little more? Anyone can work in a coffee shop."

I looked at him out of the corner of my eye and said, "I want to work in the coffee shop and I'm not interested in making any more money."

"You can always come work for me," he replied.

I tuned him out. I would not work for him. He wanted to control me and dictate to me the way he did when I was a little kid tossing a football.

He ignored my ignoring him and said, "Do you realize that you could make a lot of money as a sales associate?"

I tuned back in and started laughing inside. "What would I be selling?"

He looked away from me and said, "Well, you would sell odds and ends to grocery stores."

I chuckled (which I knew would irritate him) and said, "I don't think so."

The job didn't sound so bad (What the heck are odds and ends?) but I would never work for my father. I had done it before and he was too controlling. I would end up being a flunky for him and we would just yell at each other all the time.

We made our way into the hospital and visited my sister. The anaphylactic reaction stuff is scary. (My sister carries an EpiPen with her so that she can give herself a shot if she has an allergic reaction.) Her wind pipe was swollen and she didn't feel like talking but I could see that she would be fine.

As my father and I left the hospital, I couldn't help but look at him with sadness. I hadn't talked to him in years.

I would speak to him but there is a big difference in speaking to someone and talking with them. He wasn't the same after he announced his affairs. He didn't feel sorry for his actions and it drove us kids crazy. He was so far gone into a world of money and power and girlfriends that he had lost the ability to build honest friendships the way that I could.

We were driving on I-70 and went by an old Keebler Cookie warehouse. It wasn't there anymore but my whole life when my folks drove past it there was a delicious smell of fresh cookies. The warehouse was huge and it felt weird to pass by it now that it was leveled. The office building that stood there now made me think of concrete and mortar. It made me feel like I was on some other planet now that the warehouse was gone. Looking up I noticed that the sky was dark and I couldn't see the clouds.

My father had been quiet for the rest of the drive. He finally said, "Toby, this is a weird question but what does that ecstasy feel like?"

I was surprised at the question. "It's hard to explain." I couldn't help but laugh to myself at the idea of a sixty year old business man rolling on 'e'.

He immediately answered with, "I don't blame you for doing this stuff. If I were your age and had all the temptations that you kids have I would do it too." Now I asked myself, what does he mean? He has been telling me all my life that I shouldn't do drugs. Is he serious? Does he think that I want to be his buddy instead of his son?

Finally, we arrived at my home and I could leave him to do his thing at his home.

When my parents separated my mom had been living at our old house while my father lived in an apartment. He talked her into letting him move back into the house so she just threw up her hands and moved into a rental. Our old house was an amazing house. The family room was a giant octagon shaped room. The house was brick with five bedrooms, four bathrooms, two family rooms, a loft area for the office, a hot tub room, a bar, and then the usual living room, dining room and kitchen/eating area. It was worth a lot except for the fact that a huge water main burst in our backyard and the whole back yard was in the process of slipping down a hill that falls 200 yards below the house. The fence that was supposed to keep it up was slowly bending toward the bottom. My parents tried to sue the city but in our society no one sues city hall and wins. The city kept delaying the lawsuit and my parents finally took a token settlement. The yard was still slipping.

My father took it upon himself to try to fix the hill and make it more valuable so he could avoid foreclosure and bankruptcy. He lied to a rental company about his ability to drive a giant Cat and tried to build a wall on the hill that was below our backyard. He was trying to make the house more valuable. Well, a business man has no business with a Cat but he couldn't be talked out of "investing my time" in the potential "money maker." He lost control of it and rolled 200 yards down the hill. He survived the crash and walked away from it. I can't imagine the horror of rolling like that. He was put in the hospital with a heart condition. His new girlfriend was with me the whole time in the hospital. She looked like Tammy Faye Bakker, who was a sleazy televangelist's wife. Her necklace had three inch gold circles all around it.

After spending many hours in the hospital when my father was hospitalized, I took some vacation time from work and went to Tucson to visit my Aunt, Uncle and my favorite cousin. My cousin was 15 years old and he and I played our guitars nonstop. The guitar for me was a challenge and it took some real dedication to be mediocre but my cousin was a natural. I played guitar and swam in their pool for seven days. I taught my cousin Rage Against the Machine songs and he loved it.

My father called me the third day I was there and he harassed me again about working with him. It was the first time I have ever yelled at my father. I flat out said, "You need to stop hounding me about work and act like my father." I was pissed when he called and I exploded. Most of the time I am a passive, mellow guy but he had pushed me over the edge while I was trying to relax with my Aunt and Uncle. They overheard my explosion and their eyes got big.

While I was in Arizona, I had a little conversation with myself. I said to myself, "That's the last time I take drugs." I just felt like I had to move on and start thinking about the future. The ecstasy thing was my 'last hurrah,' and now it was time to find a cute wife and a cute house and decent job. I had the same skills my father had with people so maybe I would be able to go to real estate school, or become a stock broker. I would volunteer my free time to worthy causes. I had strong feelings about the oppressed and even though I was always charged by fists full of rebellion I think I realized that the system would never be broken down. Anarchy is the only way to bring true financial equilibrium, but that is not a reality that can be swallowed.

I flew home after this brief vacation and enjoyed the travel time as much as I enjoyed the vacation. I love the airport. It is strange to see so many people and never see them again. I love talking to random people. You can be whoever you want.

# 7

## Gabriel

August 2003

In my search for becoming a part of civilized society, I had what I considered at the time a couple snags along the way. It had been about two weeks after my vacation when I told my mom I would come down and help out with the foster care summer party. She had become a social worker and she loved what she did. She had a chance to help orphans and abused kids in Denver and find good homes for them. In the past I had volunteered for the special events with her.

We drove to the park and as we walked up to the picnic tables we were greeted by her coworkers. They all knew me because I had helped at so many other events. There was a large gazebo where all the food was and it was a place for everyone to gather.

My favorite person was a woman named Linda. She was so much like my mom. The kindness just flowed out of her. You could see love in her eyes. She, like my mom, worked because she loved the children.

The kids started showing up with their foster

families. It became crazy fast. The Director of Foster Care had planned a ton of games for the kids to play. I wasn't the only volunteer. There were two other guys who had mentored a few of the kids. We played random games that I had never heard of. There was one game where the kids got a chance to throw water balloons at us. The foster children had fun blasting us with water balloons. There was one child that was being left out and it became my duty to hang out with him. He had been sexually abused at an early age and was now thirteen and confused about who he was and how he should act. My mom introduced me to him and we hung out. I asked him some questions about his school and about things he liked. I didn't want to say too much because if a kid is abused at an early age, the trust factor needs to be developed. It always takes time to build trust and you don't want to invade the child's space. We played with a football just tossing the ball around.

There was one kid who hadn't shown up to the party. His foster parents came late. When I was in the middle of throwing the ball my mom came over and stopped me.

She took me to meet Gabriel. Gabriel was two years old.

He was a mess. He was bandaged from head to toe with gauze. He had some rare disease where he was constantly bleeding through these huge sores all over his body. His skin wouldn't adhere. The sores were at least two inches in diameter and when you first looked at him it was a complete shock. I was timid at first but my mom pushed me. When I looked at the child's eyes I was completely wrecked. He was covered in sores and blood but his eyes were so lit up. I crouched down in front of him and introduced myself. He made eye contact with me several times and he then started laughing. He was beautiful. He was so full of life. I almost started crying at the sight of this child laughing. His eyes shone like pure crystallized joy. He made me think of my father because I knew my father was sick too; sick with a sickness that would never go away. The whole world could see Gabriel's sickness but only I seemed to be able to see my father's sickness. I paired them up immediately in my mind and cried. I thought of what Dan had said about reincarnation. I figured Dan would say Gabriel did something horrible in his past life to make him this way and God was punishing him but I could see God's grace and love in Gabriel. He had so much love to offer but he was in so much pain. Blood splattered out of his mouth when he gasped for air at times but he smiled and laughed without tears. This little child showed the kind of love that is raw and to the core. I experienced a love that was marked in a moment. He probably had a year to live, but with modern medicine his years might be stretched. My mom picked him up and held him (she knew how to handle him because she was his social worker and had even helped change his dressings). The foster parents went to get some food and left Gabriel with my mom and me.

"What's the story, Mom?"

She said that once the mom found out about the disease she left him. His little legs were completely wrapped in bandages and my mom had him sitting on her leg. I walked closer to him and asked her if it was okay to touch him.

"Sure."

I put my hands on the back of his little bandaged legs. I couldn't help but think that this child was a miracle. I guess some people are the way they are for a reason. I suppose I could have been mad at God for making a child this way but I couldn't help but think he was a gift and had a reason for being in this time and in this place. I will never forget the experience of meeting the bravest person on earth. I began composing a song about Gabriel and could hear the music in my head. That little guy was fighting and losing the battle but he loved people and didn't know how valuable his lesson was to me. If only I could shine as bright as Gabriel. If only I could touch people the way that he touched me.

When we got home we pulled into the driveway and

mom went to her car to get her daytimer. I started walking toward the door. My sister came running out the front door with tears streaming down her face. She said, "Toby, Dad is dead."

I looked at her distress and knew in my heart that she was not kidding but I said, "What?"

"Dad is dead. He died this afternoon. He had a heart attack."

Again I said, "What!" I felt nothing.

My sister, weeping, reached out for me and I held her as she said over and over, "I can't believe it."

Finally, I pulled away from her and said, "Let me tell Mom." My mom had been through so much and I wanted to take charge and help her through this.

We walked into the house and sat down. It looked like my sister had been crying all day. Her face was swollen and had red blotches all over it. I didn't cry. I didn't feel anything. I wanted only to make this easier for my mom and sister.

We waited for our mom. She walked in, saw my sister and asked, "Why are you crying? What is wrong?"

I told her to sit down and she just looked at me and said, "What's going on?"

I looked her in the eye and told her that father was dead.

She dropped her daytimer and her purse and got pale. She found the corner of the couch and slowly sat down. At that point I went to her, put my arms around her and I could feel her trembling. She had been divorced from him for three years but they had been married for thirty-five years. I held her and tried to comfort her but I didn't feel too stressed about her. She is a strong woman and I knew in my heart that she would recover from this. Would I? I still didn't feel anything.

I had seen the pain that my mom went through because he was cheating on her. What are you supposed to do when you see someone you love in pain and you know the source of the pain? Isn't it okay to turn your back on the person who is causing all the hurt? Then they die and you are supposed to feel sorry?

My mom called my brother and told him about our father. He met us the next afternoon and I could tell that he was not only stunned but that he had been drinking. My brother is a modern day Viking. He has a strong look about him. He likes sports and hangs out with other Vikings. He is the smartest person I know and although he and I are close, we are complete opposites. He is a criminal lawyer and only defends people who are poor and oppressed. He has a fist tattooed on his calf representing fighting against the man. My brother doesn't talk to people unless he trusts them. He has a crazy sense of humor and can make anyone with a brain in their head laugh for hours. He won't say a word for hours and then suddenly the funniest things are pouring out of his mouth.

My poor sister had gone to the hospital the day my father died. She was by herself and saw him lying there with no life. My father's sister was at the hospital and she stole all of my father's jewelry and money. Why would she do that? I resented her and continue to. She even told my sister that because she wasn't a blood relative that she had no right to see him. It devastated my sister and I realized that I didn't want to have anything to do with my aunt. The Chaplin allowed my sister to see my father. My sister grieved in her own way just like all of us grieved in our own way. She was angry with him and only she and God know what she said to him as she identified his body. She wrote him a letter and put it in the coffin when we buried him.

I was not crying, not angry and felt numb to the whole thing. I just couldn't believe he was gone. There were so many people to call and so many arrangements to be made. There was my mom and my brother and my sister and me -- and we were clueless about how to do a funeral.

We met with a pastor and we went to the mortuary and we called the newspaper with the obituary notice and on and on and on. After all the things were arranged, my brother started the grieving process with binge drinking and I didn't blame him. I wished that I could do that too but someone had to be sober for my mom and my sister. They needed me and I wanted to be there for them.

I kept hoping through all the preparation that we could all figure out how to deal with his death. I had to learn to forgive a dead body. I had turned my back on him when he was alive but now he was dead. Could he forgive me for turning my back on him? No! He was dead. Did that let me off the hook? Could I just go on without forgiving? No! If he was done with me I needed to be done with him. My head felt like it was going to explode. I had to learn to love my enemy. And then there was the estate.

Dealing with my father's estate was difficult. He had about seven different companies and our family was in shock. My brother took charge. He decided that he didn't want to figure it all out and he wanted to just default on the businesses. My sister and I agreed. My father had the 'Tammy Faye Bakker' girlfriend who he was in business with and we just didn't want to deal with her shit.

My father's sister, the same aunt who stole all my father's things, and her family resented us for not just opening our arms to all my father's girlfriends. We, my brother, my sister and I, were clear about what we thought about what my father did to our mom. After his infidelity my father said that his betrayal didn't reflect on us kids and it was between my mom and him. He never realized how it affected us.

The day of the funeral was strange. My aunt was livid that we were not having an open casket for my father. She said, "My family mourns with an open casket." So my brother made the decision to have an open casket. My mom did not feel that it was appropriate to sit up front with us kids. (She still loved my father and she was paying for the funeral.) Out of respect for him she sat with Mike R. and Mike P(my brother's friends) and the rest of our friends lined up on the back row of the Chapel. We reserved enough room for my aunt and all her kids and their kids to sit with us but she didn't want to. My brother, my sister and I sat in the front row with two empty rows behind us.

I couldn't believe how many people were at this funeral. There were people standing up in the back of the chapel because there was no room to sit. My father definitely touched a lot of people. I put my arm around my sister to support her and my brother put his arm on top of mine. It was symbolic. My brother wanted to take care of the family. I did not want to see my father in an open casket with his hands folded over his chest and his face pasty, but I had to look to see if he was there. As I looked at him, I remembered the ring finger of his left hand and how he was unable to move it because of an old football injury. When the pastor met with my mom, sister and brother, we told him all about my father. He used our stories during the service and I could tell that my brother and my sister were pleased with his message. I was sitting on the aisle and my sister was next to me. When the service was over, the entire church started filing by us. They all shook our hands and murmured, "I'm so sorry." "He was such a great man." "You must be just crushed." "I'm sorry." "I'm sorry." "I'm sorry." I smiled a lot. I remember standing tall. It almost was like I was chosen by God to be first in line and to stand that tall. I looked everyone right in the eye. I didn't cry through the whole ordeal. I was arrogant. I didn't like being arrogant and I didn't know where it came from. The way I held myself during the funeral showed contempt. I looked at the cross and I thought of God but I didn't see Him there. All I saw was me standing and looking at a dead body. Some random man spoke to me right after the funeral and told me, "Toby, I can see the power of God in you." If he only knew how I felt. I know now that the power of God was there and it was quiet, but at the time I was feeling only my own power.

The funeral was finally over and now it was time for what? Mourning?

After the funeral my brother and I drove alone to the gravesite. It was time to bury him. This sounds disrespectful but we started laughing, talking shit, and making random jokes. How twisted to laugh when your father is going to be put six feet under in a few minutes. It was our own personal time to stop the mournful posture we were pushed to take. It was a way to fight the expected sobriety of the situation. By the time we got to the gravesite we did indeed have tears in our eyes (from laughing). Once we got to our destination we both put sour faces on like we were devastated but I think both he and I had mourned for our father three years earlier when he rejected our mom.

That night my brother asked me if I wanted to go out with him. We went to a bar called 'The Bank,' All of my brother's friends were there. My brother was dating a pretty blonde girl. She was there with him but had a callous demeanor and appeared to be jealous. She didn't seem to want to share my brother with his friends. I sat at a full table. There were three guys that were linemen for Colorado University. It was a table full of warriors and giants. My big brother was king of that table. He had a free run. He was drinking hard and I was sitting in the corner quietly, not because I felt left out but more because I just didn't fit. At one point they noticed this and tried to get me to chug a beer but I couldn't do it. Chris, one of my brother's close friends asked me if I wanted to smoke some bud, but I wasn't in the mood and I had left that all behind me. My brother's friend Andy was there and he was not a warrior or a giant. He was a musician and he and I sat and talked about music. We talked about the Beatles and who was the best one. It was nice to talk with someone that I could connect with. There was still a lot of chugging beer. I liked my brother's friends, they all care about him and I asked his friend Mike R. to take care of him. My brother is such a big guy, with such a big quality to him and such a big heart. Everyone has hard, low moments, and I needed to know that he would be safe when I left him.

I went to the bathroom and as I was coming out my brother met me. One of his friends came up to talk to him and he abruptly excused him saying, "I am talking with my little brother."

The bar was crowded but we found a corner to talk. I asked him if he was okay. He said, "I'm fine. Don't worry about me, Toby. This is just what I have to do."

I replied, "Okay, I won't worry."

My brother looked serious at this point and he said, "I need to talk to you, Toby. You have so much fucking potential!"

I shook my head and said, "What?"

"You have so much potential!" My big brother did have something to say and he wasn't going to let me go without saying it. "I know you have been screwing around the last couple years just to piss off our father, but now you need to fucking grow up! You're just wasting your potential. Why don't you make the music stuff happen?" My brother was drunk and he was letting it all out. That was cool with me if he had to get some things off his chest.

With a half smile on my face I said, "I know."

My brother is loud and when he is angry, he is louder. He yelled, "No, you don't know. You don't know and you're just fucking wasting it." Our conversation was sort of one sided because I realized that he was right and I had wasted time and energy pissing off my father by getting into drugs and shit.

I averted my eyes and asked, "What do you want me to say?"

My brother was drunk but he is smart and he realized that he had struck a chord with me. He quietly said, "I don't mean to be a prick. It's just that you care about people in a way that I can't. You are the most open-minded person I know. You are my hero."

I didn't know what to say after that. It is hard to receive compliments from a big brother whom you have admired your whole life.

My brother is my hero and he has always been. It was shocking to see him with his defenses down and his soul exposed. He defends people who have no voice and usually have no defense. They may be drug dealers and murderers but, fuck, he is still helping them and giving them a voice.

My brother and I could always talk about books and philosophy. He tried to get me to read things. He is a big Hemingway fan while I am more of a Vonnegut type, but we liked both authors. When I was taking philosophy in college, we talked about different philosophers; who we liked and who we didn't like. (He and I both hated Hobbs.)

I was shocked that my brother, the lawyer, the competitor, my hero, was so open with me. We had always had good conversations but we had never talked with him challenging me. He has tough layers to break through, but that night the layers were gone.

The time had come for me to leave the bar. I knew then as I know now that my brother is a true warrior.

My brother had to deal with our father's death and I knew he would be safe with his friends and I knew that he loved me. I knew that we would always be there to watch after each other and our family would be okay without my father. My brother will always be my hero.

The week after my father's death was interesting. I was listening to a new album. I liked the CD because it felt like a perfect match for what I was going through. Some of the songs were like a slap in the face and other songs made me think of my father and his death. It felt like all the songs were written for me because I twisted the lyrics. I had just finished reading 'The Alchemist' before my father's death and the omens that he saw stuck with me. It sort of freaked me out. I liked the beginning of the book about how a person is looking at their reflection in a lake and is consumed by it, engulfed by the lake. Self absorption is a hard thing and I think everyone is guilty of it; especially me.

It occurred to me that I was a ticking time bomb.

# Part II

**Choking on the Flood**

# 8

## Man vs. Nature

I woke up and I felt good. I was fully awake when I opened my eyes. The clock said 12:00 and it made me think of the twelve apostles of Christ. I thought about how the Gospels were written by different men but the accounts were the same. The room was brighter than usual. The alarm clock and the window had a slight neon tint, which made me open my eyes wide. Religion woke up with me. I didn't realize it but my father's death had brought up many questions and I was seeking the truth about religion and how it fit in my life.

A few days had passed since the funeral and I had been in a daze. I was in shock with all the events that had transpired. My father was dead and I hadn't shed a tear. I didn't know why. I was a stone. I'm usually the guy that cries in movies.

That afternoon I took a walk, headed toward my little park. There is a gate to access the park from the parking lot. The gate was hard to open and I struggled to shut it. I seemed to have more energy and the walk through the park was different than before. Usually my head was up and I was looking at the scenery but my head was down and I was focused on the walk.

I looked at Clear Creek fifteen feet below, through the cracks of the wooden boards on the long bridge where I stood. I had the urge to walk but I didn't know where. I kept going upstream and walked the path beneath another bridge. The trees reminded me of a dream I had of a tree carrying industrial things. The tree was walking and carrying Coors beer. It felt right because where would industry be without nature? The tree was large and the image of it was greater and finer than any ideas of man. Industry needs nature but nature doesn't need industry.

Clear Creek was calm and looked like a pristine painting. You could walk for a mile up stream. The trail ended at a large park with a recreation center. I walked to the middle of the park next to a gazebo that reminded me of where I met little Gabriel. I sat on the grass listening to music. There were geese everywhere. The grass was long. My mind started talking half truths about my father. My father and the Lord were holding hands and walking into a crystal city. It gave me comfort. I liked the idea of my father being somewhere.

I liked to read the Bible. There was one verse that rang in my mind: the first being the last. Suddenly, I saw Jesus and me together. Neither one of us was first or last. We were together. Then we are walking in circles playing first and last, both of us trying to catch the others' heels. The picture of Him was so vivid I felt like I could touch Him. I couldn't get rid of this image. Another image took its place. *If Adam and Eve where in heaven first then in the last days there will be heaven on earth because they have to be last as well as first?*

It seemed like blasphemy to toy around with these images of first, last, right, wrong, and me. I thought of myself being stomped by Jesus because of my blasphemy. The images were there and they started playing some sadistic game in my mind requiring me to figure out how the first could be the last; images more vivid than a normal thought. The images moved faster and I got lost in them. Time passed.

The image of Jesus disappeared. It was time to go. My headphones were on and the music was loud. It was strange how so many ideas could run through my brain but at the same time I could hear music. The images came back. The sun was peeking through the clouds. I couldn't control my thoughts. *Jesus walking around in circles, but Jesus can't be last. Jesus sitting at the right hand of God. Jesus sitting at the right hand of all men which makes him the son of man? We are children of God and made in his image. Would Jesus want everyone to constantly worship Him (which would be putting Him first) or would He truly want to be last? Maybe He is here on earth and he is a homeless bum just waiting to open people's eyes. On the cross Jesus asked God: why have You forsaken me? Maybe this is a foreshadow of what Christ will go through in our world. Maybe he will be forsaken until God shows His light.*

*The world is so sick now I keep looking for a fresh breeze to cover me. I know there are religious wars all over the world. If only there could be a compromise. If only there was true separation between church and state. If you look at Judaism and Islam they are close in principle. They are two hands waiting to shake. Everyone (Christians) thinks Islam is unholy but the origin of Islam stems from Abraham. Isaac -- Ishmael; which one is the chosen one? They were half brothers and somehow the connection between the two was lost. Could we look at the holy places as something to share and something to embrace by all religions, brothers and sisters? I am thinking way too much about this.*

As I started walking the thoughts stuck with me and I started to move my feet a little faster. I looked around at the plush trees. They soothed me. I was finally settling down and things were looking mellow. I still couldn't believe my father was dead. He had such a way about him. I wish I could have told him to just back off and know that he would honor my request. I also wish I could have told him that I loved him. I guess he knew but I was so disconnected from him after he spilled his guts about his 10 year affair. I couldn't tell him that I loved him because he betrayed me. He betrayed the family.

My Mp3 player was cranked high and I turned it down. I tried to look at the sun to burn my eyes out. I looked at Clear Creek and the giant boulders that rested softly against the stream. I needed to forget my father, to carry on. Death is real. Memories are just memories. As I made my way into my apartment I wanted to do something to make humanity right. I wanted to make a difference. I wanted to taste a piece of truth. If only the world would stop judging each other.

I took a knife and cut a gash on my arm. It was so real to see the blood boil out of my skin just like it could be real to stop judging a man's heart. I wore a long shirt to work to hide the gash on my arm. I can't believe I cut myself. I am falling into a pit and I can't control it.

# 9
## Stepping into Psychosis

**M**y days off were so relaxing. I wanted to watch a movie. I got in my car and put in a CD that talked about sailors. As I drove, I thought about my friends; Kelly and Caleb, and all my brother's friends, out at sea stinking of bait. It was a pleasant thought. I stopped to see my friend Lisa. We sat outside the coffee shop and had a cigarette in the alley by the dumpsters. She started talking about our friend Zane and how worried she was about him.

"I know, Lisa, but he has to make his choices."

"I know he does but he parties so hard."

"Yeah, but Zane can handle it. I don't know anyone who can drink as much as him and still act sober."

"I guess you're right, but what is he going to be like in five years?"

"I don't know. Maybe screwed up and maybe okay. How are you doing with the whole father thing?"

"It's amazing, Lisa, I haven't cried and I'm just chilled out. It's weird."

"Well, I know your circumstances are weird."

"I will get over it if I can get through it."

"I'm going back inside, my ten minutes are up."

I needed to talk to a friend, but Lisa had to get back to work. I got in my new car and I was off. When I need some good down time I watch movies. I think it's funny that in our world our highest honor is bestowed on people who act like someone else. On my way to the video store, I saw a liquor store. I know they say people who drink by themselves are alcoholics, but I needed it.

After the liquor store I stopped by a video place. I was still feeling anxious and I was looking for something to help me mellow out. I saw a video that said, "There is still hope." *There was a shining gloss around the cartridge and it looked like it was alive. I guess there is still hope.*

I left the video store in a daze. I felt like the videos were talking to me. I got in my car and I started playing a CD. Elliot Smith sang, Between the Bars: "Drink up baby, stay up all night with the things you could do, you won't but you might. The potential you'll be that you'll never see. The Promises you'll only make. The People you've been before."

*What the fuck is going on, yeah, I will drink up. I will stay up all night with the things I could do, I won't, but I might. The potential I'll be that I'll never see?*

*This song is fucked up. Why is everything around me talking to me? My brother thinks I have potential, but for what? To work my way up and make a shit load of money and have a wife and kids. Maybe that isn't what I want and maybe it is. My brother wants me to be successful but I think he would rather see me happy. Does success define happiness? I think if you accept who you are no matter what you can be happy.*

The line in the song, "The people you've been before that you don't want around anymore," hit me hard because of some ideas of reincarnation I had. *The differences in each person's soul makes me think that our spirits have been around forever and maybe we choose who to be in our next life based on the limitations of the world and God.*

All the CD's I've been listening to lately seemed to be talking to me.

I drove home and the anxiety continued. Something in me said to go further. I had to watch the video even though I was freaking out.

I started watching the movie. I thought about palaces and movie stars who were once in these huge mansions that are now empty. The movie was depressing. It was about what happens with success. Most of the movie stars that were so well known have turned to ash and are forgotten. Some people remember them but the majority look ahead to what is new and exciting. I wonder if the same thing will happen to the actors of today. These important people have everything and maybe one day they will be forgotten. Thank God the movie wasn't talking to me.

The sun was starting to set and there was a blue light that permeated my apartment. I felt reckless. I wondered what heroin felt like. Elliot Smith did heroin. I had never done it, but I wondered. I had an overweight friend that sold me some pot in college. He got into heroin. I didn't see him for a semester. When I saw him he was skinny. His mom was with him and it looked like she was trying to help him.

*The blue gazed shadow and the movie drip like the afterglow and I start breathing heavy. I keep breathing deeper and deeper when suddenly energy from outside my body starts pushing on me. At this moment my chest and body completely relax. My anxiety is there and this energy starts making my body feel high. I keep breathing in and I can't help but laugh.*

*What the fuck is going on?*

*I can't control it and suddenly I stop worrying about everything. I relax and enjoy where I am. I know something isn't right with me but I am not quite sure what to do other than enjoy the moment. Maybe tomorrow will be different. Maybe tomorrow I will feel a little better. I wish I hadn't taken that ecstasy. I wish I hadn't smoked so much pot.*

# 10
## Flash of White

The days seemed to run endlessly by. It was hard to remember things. It had been two weeks since my father's death. I went to see my niece, Jayde. It kept coming back to me how I've had a father/uncle relationship with her since she was born. It is strange to feel like a father but to have no responsibility. I was in my second year of college when she was born. When I left Greeley, where I went to school at the University of Northern Colorado, and moved back to Denver for a second chance at school I had an opportunity to spend a great deal of time with her and my sister and my mom. I was closer to her than her father ever had been. As I walked through the door a four year old came running up to me and greeted me her usual way, wrapping her arms around my leg.

I asked her if she would like to read our book. She said, "YES" and I grabbed her and the book, "Where the Sidewalk Ends" by Shel Silverstein. She loved the book for the pictures. Her favorite was the one where the dentist was pulling the tooth of an alligator. We relaxed and read and before we knew it we had finished the book. I always skipped a few pages here and there so that she wouldn't get bored. It was our little ritual and I loved seeing her respond to the strange voices I made to imitate the characters.

My mom and sister were in the kitchen when Jayde and I finished reading. We, Jayde and I sat on the couch watched cartoons. Then the strangest thing happened. The cartoon characters were talking to me. I associated each character with people in my life and the icons that I was familiar with. Before I knew it the story was different. I looked at Jayde and felt frustrated. What was going on? I got up and went into the kitchen, leaving Jayde with the deranged cartoons.

"How are you?" I asked my mom.

My mom, who is usually together says, "Oh, I'm okay. I guess I'm still a little frustrated and sad. How are you, Hon?"

I looked at both my mom and my sister and said, "I don't know, I just feel like the world is falling in on me."

My sister sighed and said, "I know how you feel. I still can't believe it. How could he leave us before he told us he loved us more than his new life?"

My frustration was building and I knew that my mom and my sister had no clue about what was going on with me. I just nodded at my sister and said, "It's something more. I feel a little weird."

Jayde walked in with a serious expression on her face. She asked, "What color is your heart, Gramma?"

My mom smiled and answered, "Red."

Jayde smiled and said, "Gramma, your heart is brown and Mommy, your heart is pink."

I asked her, "What color is your heart, Jayde?"

She replied, "Purple, and your heart is black, Booie."

Whoa, I thought. Jayde started talking more and her words cut me. It felt like she was seeing deep inside of me. Her words rang true. Every word she said seemed to reflect a part of me. I was trying to get her words to make sense; maybe there were deep truths hidden there for me.

I asked her if she wanted to go outside and play in the backyard. She jumped up and down with delight. We ran in circles around a tree and when I caught her I tickled her and threw her up in the air. I was happy. The times when Jayde and I played always made me feel happy. I liked kids, but I loved this one. She and I ran around until we both got tired. We went back inside and I realized that it was time to go to work.

The music in the car was too much for me so I turned the radio off. When I got home I dressed for work. I was scheduled to close the store. I walked to the coffee shop and started my nightly ritual. Dan, the 'reader' came in. He had the same spit collected in the corner of his mouth and I was tired of listening to his garbage. He was a person who didn't listen to you, he only spouted off his stuff. I thought of my father. I talked to him but never talked with him. Strange! My father always said, "Toby, a good listener is a good learner." He never listened.

I'd had my horoscope read once at a party so Dan wasn't the first reader to try to define me. The girl that read it was cool about it. She had listening skills that most people don't. I had been playing guitar the whole night when the girl stepped up to me and started talking about my artistic abilities. She defined me according to what she had observed that night.

Dan, the swine, hit me hard when he defined me. He told me I was a teacher. That was something that I would have loved to do. I just couldn't find the passion to go back to school.

Dan started talking. He was telling me about all the crazy things that he saw when he was a kid. He told me a story about how he saw a crazy person in a cell reading the Bible twenty-four hours a day. In my eyes he was telling me that according to him that is where I should be. I was not afraid to tell people like him about my own beliefs as long as they would listen. Dan has listened to me but on this day it felt like he was mocking me.

He finally left and Lisa and I were left alone in the coffee shop. We started talking about Dan. I always talked shit about him because he was always turning what you said into an argument. He wasn't talking to you; he was just trying to get a rise out of you. He reminded me of my grandfather. My grandfather was 91 years old and his only joy in the world was arguing with people. I loved him and would try to listen to him but he was narrow-minded. I didn't blame him for trying to always spark a debate. I think he was just bored. My mom was raised in a super conservative environment where all they ever did was study, talk, and argue about the "END" according to Bible prophecy.

The afternoon moved on and suddenly a pretty girl walked in. She drank an Irish cream latte and she was cool in a rugged sort of way. I talked with her at the espresso bar while I made her drink, and on my break I sat with her. She told me about a book she was reading about a girl who was looking for a shepherd, finds him, and falls in love. Her words about the book were spoken for me. *Maybe I am the shepherd.* There was something in the air. She had dark skin and had a strong desire to make some kind of difference in people's lives. We kept talking and I got her telephone number. Her name was Diana. Our conversation was marked with deep, pensive looks and we were flirtatious, but cautious.

"So, you said you went to Metro for a marketing degree? What does a Marketing Degree get you?"

"You know, I've been asking myself that same question. It seems like a waste because I still haven't found a job that has anything to do with marketing. What are you studying?"

"Psychology. In order for me to do anything with psychology though, I will have to get a masters degree and that seems like a lot of work. But, I like school and I like a challenge."

I looked at this attractive girl and said, "You know, I could never study psychology because I would think that I had every psychosis I ever learned about. I would probably end up treating myself in some remote mental hospital."

She smiled and said, "No, you wouldn't."

*Suddenly a flash of white! I opened my eyes wide and thought, what the fuck?*

I regained my composure and grinned back at her saying, "So, what do you do with your time when you are not studying psychology?"

Her intensity level rose and she said, "I go to an awesome church and am quite active in it. Are you religious?"

I was taken aback by her brashness, but honored her question.

"You know, religion is a funny thing. I was raised in the church but now feel like I go to church when I'm with my friends. You know, we kind of have a pulse. We have no fear of being honest with each other. Sounds strange, but it's better than having someone telling me a one sided story; however, I do go to church occasionally." The preacher at my church is honest, which makes for interesting sermons.

She seemed to respect what I had said.

"Are you in a relationship now?"

She smiled at me and answered, "No, I don't have the time for a relationship."

Things were getting a little sticky so I asked her about her past relationships.

She told me that she was in a lesbian relationship. I just stared at her. She trailed off after that and talked about how religion had changed her and her ideas about what relationships should be.

Everything about her struck me and as I watched her leave. I hoped to get a date with her. She had a bright green VW Jetta and as the days passed I saw her often. I called her a few times and left messages but she called me back only once. She still came in and we talked. She was a hardcore Christian girl and talked about her church. Her style was unique and several of my coworkers thought she was crazy because she talked about her faith.

During the time when she talked to me I got lost in white pillars where all I could see were flashes of white in my head. It was like a slice of white that hit me and kept coming. I caught myself waiting for the white and then staring at it. They were forces of something seeping its way into me. I thought I might be having a nervous breakdown. I saw the white when I was doing random things. It was frustrating. I just didn't feel right and I had stopped eating.

The night after my first conversation with Diana was unforgettable. I had a dream that I lived with people in huts and caves on a mountain. I was trying to tell them that water was coming up the mountain and they needed to follow me. They sounded German and they didn't understand me. I was so afraid of the water and the flood that was coming that I left them. I ended up at the top of a mountain waiting for the water to rise. I was frightened at first but then looked at the horizon and calmness came over me. I knew I was going to die but I faced it. When the water was almost touching me I dreamt of becoming a whale. I asked God to make me a whale because I didn't want to be human and I knew that if I could be a whale I would still be alive. When I finally woke I was in a panic.

The rest of the day was foggy and the dream was like a vision. I could see it more vividly than any dream I had ever had. I couldn't shake it. I walked to work and saw Dan. I still had a few minutes so I talked to him. I told him my dream knowing he would judge me because of it but hoping that he could explain it. I was asking for wisdom from a man who chases stars. He couldn't explain the dream. He had no clue what I was even talking about. I came to the conclusion that I was just feeling overwhelmed and needed to relax about the dream. It took some time but I finally put the dream to rest.

My sister was having a birthday party for Jayde after work and I found myself driving but not conscious of how I got to their house. My whole family was there. I saw Colin and Amanda (Amanda is my cousin) with their kids and some other friends of my sister's. The house that my mom, sister and Jayde lived in was nice. As I made my way into the house I felt like a cow being brought in for slaughter. I was tired and felt two steps behind on everything that was going on. Colin asked me how I was doing with my father's death and I told him I was doing just fine. It was amazing how good of an actor I was. He said that he thought that my big brother would have the hardest time dealing with it. I could have told him that I was fucked up but I didn't.

The party was pink! It was disgusting. It was everywhere. Jayde opened all her presents, and after she was finished, everyone went to the kitchen and I was left sitting with my niece playing Barbies in this horrid pink palace. I was tied to this room and I couldn't move. I had to sit there. It was like the room was some strange box of pink and I couldn't escape it. Something came over me as I listened to this little girl that I loved. She became more distant. Suddenly, I saw us in a dark pink pit. I knew it was hell because I couldn't move. There was pink everywhere and I was locked into a pink cell. I tried to play with her but I couldn't. She was playing with her Barbies. She talked to them and threw them around. I knew I could now move but something dark in the room was holding me there. My brother came in and saved me from whatever pink hell I had created. He asked me if I wanted to go get some beer and the shackle around my brain was broken.

My brother and I sat in his car and I told him how fucked up I was and that I couldn't explain it. I told him that I thought I had done something wrong and was being punished because of my contempt for God. I didn't explain to him the ecstasy night and the demons I was wrestling that night. He laughed and said, "Toby, there are things in my life that I truly regret too, but I got over it." We kept driving and our father was not mentioned. We started talking about Christianity and the afterlife. It is amazing how when someone close to you dies suddenly, the subject of afterlife comes up.

I said to him, "Look at what organized religion has done to the world."

He looked at me and said, "Toby, I know this! But what Jesus stands for is something worth looking at. I don't know about my beliefs sometimes but I know if I follow my path (it might not be the same as others) I still have the framework."

I sensed in my brother someone who had fought his own demons in the same way I was fighting mine. As we walked in the door I said to him, "You are so much like the Apostle Peter. Just the way you are and how you deal with things."

He just laughed.

The night dragged on. We decided to help my mom move some furniture, but I was so spaced out that I couldn't concentrate. I asked my brother several times, "Is this where I should put the chair?"

He responded with a calloused, "What is wrong with you?" He couldn't see that I was lost in my own confusion.

The party was over and I gave Jayde a hug and a kiss before I went home. When I got home, I turned the TV on and watched a PBS special about rockets. They went through all the science of building them, which I couldn't follow but it was still interesting. Watching those rockets go into space reminded me of a time when I was downtown with my friend Dustin.

Dustin is a good looking, tall guy who was a lot like me. He and I played Hendrix and Beatles on our guitars. We tried to start a band at one time but we had the same blocks. The dream we had was to write music that affected people because it was different. We usually talked about the dream more than we worked on it. We had a drummer and a bass player who were talented but when it came to singing neither of us had the training or the balls to just spit it out. The drummer said we sounded like 'Hootie and the Blowfish,' which was okay except the drummer was a total prick and said it in the most condescending way possible. I wanted to tell him to get the fuck out of my house, but of course I didn't.

As for the rockets, Dustin and I were downtown and we had a few drinks in us. As we walked from our car, we encountered a crippled, homeless guy. He had a long ZZ Top beard and he was an interesting guy. He was telling us how one day, after an accident, an angel grabbed him and shot him up like a rocket to a place he couldn't describe. Dustin and I were both young and the way the man told the story was amazing. He had such an honest look. He freaked both Dustin and I out completely. I asked, "What happened when you were in this place?" He explained that God talked to him, not in a voice but more like directly to his brain. Then the homeless guy said that he was sent back to earth to stop homelessness and that was his purpose. We talked for a good while more and Dustin gave him all his cash. I didn't have much on me but I gave him some smokes. Dustin and I walked on to a swanky bar on 16th street and talked about the whole episode.

The TV went to commercial and I was not as spaced out. The next program was a tribute to Martin Luther King. I love documentaries and I love to see a preacher who is passionate and real. They showed many clips of him, but the one that stood out was one of him talking about working. The words went so fast. It was something about how a man in a position of mopping floors or doing hard labor should take his mop and with every stroke give it to God and praise Him and love him. That kind of counsel is so compelling. I thought about the idea and I wished I could give God that. At the coffee shop we sweep and mop the floors every night and clean the bathrooms. I was thinking while watching the Martin Luther King tribute of my father and wishing I could have had a father that had that kind of wisdom. I wish I'd had a wise father who had an actual relationship with his son and not just a nag pushing him to be great in sports or to follow in his footsteps in the great corporate world where supposed greatness lies. I guess I saw in Martin Luther King someone who had overcome adversity and someone who had learned how to face things.

The next day at work sweeping the floor, I tried to give honor to God with each stroke of my broom. I tried to love Him in it. I listened to the customers' conversations as I swept. There were students from the School of Mines, joking and laughing. In the corner I saw an engineer. He was writing calculations. I saw a couple who were sitting awkwardly across from each other. I pushed the broom some more and I started hoping for something better than this.

I hoped for a place or a path that I could find on my own, which would give me challenges and joy. I had sent out quite a few resumes since I graduated and nothing had come from it. It seemed a college degree meant nothing and it was all about who you knew not what you knew. I guess that is the nature of the beast. After I swept, I stood behind the counter and tried to find smiles. I found a few after I acted like a clown. There is something powerful in a smile and somehow that was the only satisfaction I had when the day was done.

After work my friends took me out. I guess they all knew that the father thing was sort of hanging over my head. Kelly, Karlee, Millie, Mary and I all went downtown to the Rio. The Rio was a swanky bar with tons of yuppies, but the drinks were extra strong and good. The more booze I put in myself the more I lost the feeling that the people talking to me were telling me some big truth. We moved on to a dance club and I danced a little. My friends teased me because I was doing a hippy dance to hip hop but, what the hell, that was the only way I could dance.

I was thankful for the friends. I started getting a sense of arrogance about how loved I was by my friends. It filled me. I sat down close to the edge of the floor on a stump. As I sat there watching everyone my head felt like it was touching the ceiling and contempt along with recklessness made me sit tall. It was the same arrogance that I felt at my father's funeral.

I talked with Karlee. Her words got mixed up and I heard her talking about arrogance. The bells rang in my mind and it felt like she was choking me. It felt like she was mocking me and could see my arrogance. I didn't like her seeing the arrogance in me and I didn't feel like me anyway. I was caught up in some sick game. There are so many arrogant people in the world. My father was an arrogant man. He was a business man standing by a fire pit wanting warmth from his money. I suppose there are many business men seeking warmth from their money. I went home and went to sleep knowing my eyes would be closed and I would feel nothing in a deep silent sleep.

# 11

## The Artist

I worked the next day and tried to breeze through it. During my long silent sleep the night before, I'd had a dream. I was locked in a dark garden. The shrubbery that had been alive, now, was dead. The gates had vines crawling up them and Dan and Alex were standing outside the gate making clicking noises, like some sort of demonic language. The noises sounded unnatural and Dan and Alex just stood there staring at me. The darkness was stronger than the black background. They wouldn't stop making that horrible noise. I couldn't shake the dream and it made work a horror.

We had a new guy at the coffee shop who talked a lot. He was speaking backwards and it felt like he could read my mind. I didn't want to be near him. He had a huge scar across his face and working with him made the day not only a day of horror but also a day of fear.

I had extra energy when I left work and I walked home. Kelly, my roommate, was there with Karlee. They were a good couple and I always liked hanging out with them. Kelly grabbed a CD and put it on. Kelly didn't play the guitar too well because he didn't practice, but he and I sat around occasionally and jammed. We grabbed our guitars and figured out the music on this particular song quickly. A few years earlier, I was not able to listen to a piece of music and figure it out by ear but now it came easily. We tried working on another song, which was a challenge because the single notes were strong and I couldn't figure out the chord progression. I eventually got it when Karlee and Kelly were in the kitchen. Kelly was making dinner for them and as I walked in I asked him what he was making. He was making some sort of chicken thing and he asked me if I wanted some. I declined. For some reason I had stopped eating. I was smoking a lot and that seemed to be my only nourishment. He then asked me if I had heard of some new band that had just issued a new CD. I said no so he put the disk in the CD player. It had a perfect feel to it. After dinner I asked him if I could burn the CD to my mp3 player.

It was starting to get cold so I grabbed my black hoodie. Fall was coming soon and the night air had a moist chill about it. My last name is printed on the manufacturing tag of the hoodie because my father had been marketing his own line of clothing. He was proud of his name and since he was now dead, I was proud to wear it. It's hard to forgive someone when they aren't there to talk to, but I was trying.

The darkness of a dream the prior night spilled into my day, but the darkness of the night had open arms. As I took a step outside the music started. I didn't know why I had such a strong urge to walk but I did. It was about the time when most people go to bed. I walked and thought about my father and the afterlife. I thought of all the religions in the world and how I wished I knew more about them. I walked through my little park and my mind continued to wander. I thought about conversations I'd had about the devil. People like Dan, the astrologer, think of the devil as this scary guy covered in scales. People forget that the devil, at one time, was favored most by God.

*Sympathy for the devil. If there are angels, if you saw him, he would be amazing looking. In all the prophecies how could someone tell whether an angel was good or bad? God allows what he allows. Is the devil just a manifestation of mans' sin? Maybe there is no heaven or hell. The devil and hell aren't talked about much in the Bible. It is the propaganda fear element that makes people so afraid of it. If hell is eternal fire what does fire do? It destroys so maybe hell is the extermination of the soul.*

I recalled a friend telling me that if he was going to hell, then I was too. I laughed as I walked. I thought of reincarnation and some kind of constant flow on this earth; the search for enlightenment. Maybe the one life you live is God's gift. I kept moving and the reincarnation thing kept recurring in my thoughts. I had studied it once. The thing that had awed me about the nature of the world was how every seed made its own mark.

*In the dark space where there are no eyes watching, I can't help but dance to the music. I dance in circles. There is a free step in my feet and I wonder what I look like. I know there are no eyes. The exposed night is unequal to the masks covering the day.*

I made my way to my apartment and stood in the doorway. I looked out at the night. I danced like a reckless wrecking ball, one man dancing in the wind trying to mop the pavement and trying to understand what God wants from me.

# 12

## Lost

**W**hen I got off work the next day, I was still scared that I was not right. The night before I had felt so connected and I wanted to push on. I had this energy to look for truth (or bury myself). I realized the search for truth was the journey I had to take. I felt there were chemicals in my head pushing me. I wanted to stop walking and find a good job and live a normal life, but I was being pushed and I liked the feeling, the same way a druggy likes his drugs. I came home and started reading the Bible. I had contempt building as I sat there on the couch searching for truth. Why are we here in this life? Why are things so hard? There are people in the world that suffer in horrific ways and I am listening to backwards talkers and dancing in the night without knowing how someone feels who is in real poverty. I don't know what to do so my feet keep taking me places. I look like a ghetto guy with my hoodie but my free-wheeling legs are making me do circles and I'm driven to learn something. It makes me turn pages. What a clown. I put down the Bible then I picked it up again. I went to the book of Daniel and Isaiah where prophesy about the Messiah is written. I was engrossed in it and then I saw Dan laughing at me. I didn't care. I had to dig a little. I saw the contradiction about Christ being the Messiah. A spot sparkled; it sort of freaks me out and I throw the Bible down.

I walked out the door, jumped in my Jeep and I wondered what challenge the night might bring. I put Johnny Cash in the CD player. I thought of the time when my father took me to see him in concert when I was about 14. I was into heavy metal and sort of leery about listening to country but he was, after all, Johnny Cash. I remember seeing all the rockabilly guys walking around. Johnny put on a good show with his wife, June Carter Cash. I always dug the song 'The Circle Won't be Broken'. I don't think Cash wrote it, but I have heard him sing it. As I was driving I listened to 'A Boy named Sue.' I remembered going to the mountains to see Grandpa Tolini when we were kids and my brother and I would both want to get the Johnny Cash CD out. My father was always excited that my brother and I liked Johnny Cash. It was a connection we had. I lost my enjoyment for watching sports but sports had been the main connection with my father. I still watched a game now and then and I guessed that my brother would take me to a couple of Broncos games since he now had my father's season tickets. I go with him in the Tolini tradition, but more to spend time with my brother than to watch the game.

Another day passed of not working. I found myself hanging out with Caleb and Andrea, my old friends from college. They didn't know about the bad chemicals in my head. Caleb and I, of course, had too many drinks. I had fun with them because we share both good and bad memories. It was strange to see them married. Caleb had a great job and Andrea was still beautiful and full of fun. They deserved the best in this world. I wished I could be so relaxed and normal. I felt like I had turned into a monster.

The visit with my old friends was over and I drove home along the foothills looking at the mountains I had seen so many times before. I felt angry that the world was the way it was. I also felt like my heart hurt. Not in a physical way. Why did God make it so hard for me? I have so much to be thankful for but the days drug on with confusion and doubt invading my mind. I thought, maybe I could start working for a non profit; maybe I could do some volunteering. As I kept driving I got the sense of how lost I was and how much I would love to do something good for somebody. If my friends and family were talking they would say I am doing good things, but what I have done doesn't mean anything in the world. What I am means nothing in the world.

When I arrived home I was alone. I looked out the window and didn't see Kelly's car. I walked into the bathroom and looked at myself. I wanted to see what I was.

I remembered one time when Caleb and I took a quarter sack of pot and put it in a brownie mix. We found the recipe on the Internet and added more pot than the recipe called for. We both thought the brownie stuff was bullshit and it couldn't get you high. When we were mixing it, we followed the directions perfectly except for the extra pot we added. We cut it in four pieces and as we ate the first piece I looked over at him and stuck out my tongue. It was covered with pot. We waited about a half hour after eating it and nothing happened. (I guess it takes a full hour to go into effect.) We decided to eat the last two brownies. Another half hour passed and then it hit me like a freight train. I was walking around the house saying, "I can't find myself." I looked in the mirror and there was nothing there. It freaked me out and I told Caleb that I may need to go to the hospital because I am not here anymore. He laughed and we played cards to calm me down.

So I stood there on this different night looking at myself. I felt angry. Angry because I didn't seem to be able to do more to help people that needed help. I didn't know how I could help, but I wanted to. Before I knew it the bad chemicals did something and something shot out of my mouth so fast that I couldn't hold on to it. Hard words that break boards were flying out of my mouth.

*"Why am I here, God?*
*What do you want from me?*
*I don't know where I fit. I am lost!*
*I hate my heart! I hate it!*
*I hate the heart you gave me!*
*I am sick of caring!*
*I am sick of caring!*
*I don't fucking want it anymore!*
*Why can't I be a person that doesn't care!*
*I hate my heart! Do you hear me! I hate it!"*

I was sitting in my dirty bathroom and my body was throbbing. I was screaming at myself in the mirror. I walked out of the bathroom and sat on the couch. I was alone and I didn't have the will to follow through with doing anything other than walking. (The next day Kelly told me that he was in his room and he told me that he thought there were three people in the bathroom screaming. It scared the shit out of him.) I felt bad for freaking him out but I was in a moment of finding truth, so I brushed it off.

# 13

## The Breaking Point

The night snuck through like a river feeding into the ocean. The streets and pathways were calling my name, so I followed. I grabbed my headphones and my black hoodie and started walking. I had energy all around me. Before I knew it, I was running as fast as I could. I could feel my legs burning, but I just had to run, to feel the burn. I had to burn it out of me.

I walked back and sat on a ten foot by ten foot beach in front of an apartment building along Clear Creek. There was a big rock that I was leaning against and I looked up at the apartments across the stream. The apartments reminded me of Amsterdam. I loved how all the buildings looked like they were tipping over.

*Maybe I can't find answers for myself. Maybe some people are destined to be lost.*

I decided to go home and read a little more Scripture. I never had been drawn to it like this and I didn't want to open the Book, but I did it like my hands weren't my own.

I read and then went for a walk. The night had just started.

I was led by music again and my feet kept moving. I was pissed off that my father had left me with sharp memories. I thought about my friends and how so many felt left out. I kept walking. I didn't feel like stopping.

*How could anyone have sympathy for the devil? So many bad chemicals. God made everything for a reason. A man can choose his will. A man goes where his conscience leads him. The arrogance of the devil is why he is where he is.*

So much flying around in my head.

*Everyone has an angel with him. First is last and last is first. I can see me and my angel falling because I show sympathy to the devil.*

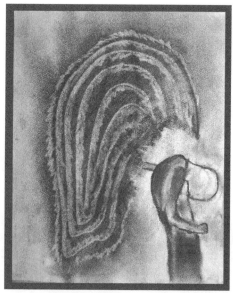

*What if the devil is the harsh beating of a man's conscience and because there is beating and punishment he fights his conscience?*

*Maybe the Holy Spirit is everyone's angel and they are helping man and woman. What if there is no God, or no right or wrong?*

My head hurts. Fuck the world for making me like this. I was such a kind, smart person, but now my wits are dulled chasing trite questions. What leads me to these questions? I don't want to be lost anymore!

Numbers in my head. They seem to build on each other. The numbers tell it all and each number represents something.

*I am sitting with the devil in hell.*

*The monsters are coming.*

I have to walk, to stop thinking, to chill out.

*What if the devil is Jesus' angel but Jesus doesn't know it? If the first is the last in heaven the devil and Jesus would match up.*

My thoughts are disrespectful.

*Father, Son, Holy Spirit (devil). Three. Three times two is six. Fuck that, I am not six six six antichrist. No threes. There is the Father, Son, Holy Spirit, and the devil. Fours. Fours are the way to go. Three-no, four-yes! Three four three four three four.*

*The monster is coming and it is me! Three, four, cut off the zeros. What is the equation? Everything in fours is good and threes are bad.*

Why am I in this mix of panic? I have to stop digging, but I can't.

*How many ends on the cross? Four. Go with fours.*

My mind keeps thinking way too fast. Stop thinking so much. Chill out. I walk by a 7-11.

*7, 11, 7, 11, that isn't bad, it isn't 3 so it is ok. 7, 11, 7, 7, 7, 11, 11, 11.*

I went in the store for a pack of smokes. I see drinks that have threes and avoid them and then find comfort in the drinks that say four. I buy a bottle of water and continue walking. I realize that Christianity is based on faith. I keep walking. I have to think this through.

*What if the first is the last so men are guided by their own truth or conscience- the alpha and omega- the beginning and the end? Maybe we are all stuck in the middle waiting to see the first and the last. Maybe there is a simple way to explain it.*

*Could all religions be truth and everything everyone believes shed slivers of gold. As far as truth is concerned, say, a man says, "I hate my brother." Whether or not he hates his brother-- two ideas exist. Loving your brother and hating your brother. There are two ideas, but truth is still alive. Religion is so messed up. It kills and scars so many individuals around the world. Maybe all religion is a joke and a way to keep us locked in our subconscious.*

*Pictures of crosses in my head. All the churches that buy enormous crosses. Aren't those just idols? If people need a reminder of the sacrifice why spend all the money that people tithe on making idols. Why not put two small pieces of wood at the entrance of the church and stop wasting money on big crosses. All the pictures that people look at and pray to. Isn't that idol worship, and wouldn't Jesus be pissed about that? As a child in church I looked at the giant cross and prayed to it instead of to God. Why build their buildings? The life Christ lived was humble. People stare at the cross to remember to worship but forget the life of Jesus and how humble He was. I am guilty. He conquered the cross and He rose up. What would Jesus do if he saw people worshiping the cross or worshiping the picture they have of him hanging on the wall? Our prayers should be "our Father who art in heaven hallowed be thy name." We are supposed to pray to God and not to Jesus. Jesus is the sacrifice and gives the gift of redemption. I don't think he would want us to pray to the pictures in our head of him. We have to find him in our heart. What about the big beautiful cathedral with his picture plastered everywhere? I bet he would burn down every fucking brick of every fucking cathedral and every fucking lavish church and give the money to the poor. I dream of broken bricks and broken wood. Jesus would feel wonderful if He went to a man's house and that man had given all his tithes to orphans and the downtrodden instead of giving to the "Church" for a big tax write-off.*

*Why am I preaching to myself? Preachers get salary raises and perks from the members of their church and the preacher talks and talks and talks while the poor and down trodden are still hungry and lonely and cold. I think a man's heart would beat like a drum if he knew his money wasn't going to raise people's salaries or build bigger buildings, but was instead going to people who needed help. I should find a church like that. The pastor of the church I go to is always talking about stepping over the line to get to Jesus. That is crazy. A man's heart and where he chooses to go is the true soul of a man and no one on the outside can know anyone's heart. No buildings can break the will to overcome sins of the conscience. They always show themselves. In the Christian Bible, God says He will look at each man according to where he comes from. Everyone judges. I guess when someone walks into a room they look at a person and decide who that person is. It is the people who act on their judgment that are in the wrong. But to judge an idea is not to judge a man.*

The night is still even with all the confusion in my brain and I think about my Mammy (my Mom's Mom) who was so deep into religion. She was plagued by it her whole life. I can feel her pain and her wanting for something better. My confusion about the world and the backward talking makes me feel close to her. Did she think these same thoughts? Looking at the stars my eyes well up. I know her struggle and I feel close to her.

I have to work tomorrow and the sun is coming up. I don't know how I stayed up all night. It is so beautiful. The stars were like sprinkling balls of fire and I have this wonderment about me and I wish to see God's love with all that I am. I think of all the songs my Mom and Mammy sang. I remember watching my Mammy die and listening to the old gospel hymns my Mom sang to her as she died. It gave them both peace.

I look up in the sliced sun and I have the same feeling I've had in churches where gospel hymns ring. I can see how much God loves us and it is so beautiful. I can see and feel millions of angels singing. It is like a gift dropped down from the skies for me and I stand watching the sun come up in awe. It is spilling dreams, it is wonder seams. I can't see it but I can see it. I can feel it in my bones. I am sitting in the middle of my park and my mind is at complete rest for this moment and I think I am in heaven. I am in a strange meditation with my eyes open. Everything is clear and my mind is focused.

*Lines and shapes wrap me in a blanket of truth. The grass is moving slightly. Confusion clouds with sin but judgment is gone. I am in heaven. I am not sinning now and my mind is sharp. I see solid without any reflection of an evil thought. I might be the reincarnation of Christ because God has shown me heaven. Heaven on earth. Heaven on some distant planet. Heaven is our spirits on some other dimension. I have to tell the world that I have seen it. Jesus said to love God with all your heart. I am trying. I throw my dreams up for God. Maybe there is no God, but in one perfect moment there is. Maybe the man that walks through the door and says, "Hey" to Bob Dylan has found truth. Maybe he is still connected to the religion he grew up with. Faith is stronger than any army could ever destroy.*

I'm in my apartment and I pick up the Bible. I am not normally so obsessed like this but religion feels right to me. Dan is laughing at me. I start reading Jeremiah. I like Jeremiah. He had truth cornered and was willing to step into a crowd and say it.

*A glow. Suddenly I am what I want to be. Truth seems so strong and it is ripe off my lips and every word I read is true. I have to tell everyone. I have to speak honest words. I have answers and maybe they will listen.*

The air looks different. There is a brightness to it. I look at the clock -- 7:00. I should be at work. If I go they will think I am crazy because I can't lie anymore. I have to walk. I might lose my job but I can't go into work like this. I am going to the top of Table Mountain. It is a hike, but I have to go there. I have to make the trek. I put on an orange Broncos shirt. It has a pale white horse on it. I was born with that white horse. I think I am losing weight. I feel good in this shirt. I throw my sandals on. I grab the Bible. Maybe God wants me to speak with an honest tongue. No, I am no one important, but maybe someone will listen. Maybe He wants me to stand on two feet. My head is engrossed in the Bible and the walk up the streets of suburbia feels like a walk to a true Zen-state, or maybe I have finally found the valley of hope. I feel like I have turned into Superman -- the man of steel. I am walking on pavement and the words on the page are strong. My shirt feels good to wear. My body and muscles feel strong and are resonating.

*I can't see the words. I'm afraid. The words keep changing. "Hungry" becomes "angry," now "hungry" again. I keep turning the pages and the black lines are moving. The stem of the plants are moving all around me and it is not good. A confusion of words. I can't find the words and the words are true. I am seeing things I shouldn't see. It's happening so fast I can't control it. Trying to find the words. The feeling of triumph is now confusion. I walk and I turn the pages. I feel so alive and I see magic coming from the pages. Is it from the devil or is it the manifestation of man's sin or is it some delusion I created in my subconscious? It is dark. The ecstasy night, I let something in. It is still with me? I keep walking. I am at the trail head. I am a child looking for answers. I know there are good people in churches. The rocks are big and I take big steps. I don't understand how they can laugh in their palaces. St. Peter's Basilica where I stood in awe while there was blasphemy everywhere. The beggars outside the church. I keep walking. The trail winds around the mountain. My father is gone. His face, a bubble in my head. His unique spirit. My brother's bubble and his spirit. My sister's bubble and her spirit. Faces at the top of the mountain. The cross and Jesus are up at the top of the mountain.*

The sky has rolled back and crimson covers the mountain. I can't see it, but I feel it. The red is stretching to every corner of the mountain. I fall down in a quiver of panic. I don't want this. I don't want this. I get up and start walking at a fast pace down the mountain looking back in fear.

I have committed true blasphemy. The bubbles of seeing my father, brother and sister feel like they are shot out of my brain. It is like a shotgun hit me in the head and my brain is mush. There is quivering soaked in steady feet. There is quietness that chills me enough to want to speak something. There is sadness that pulls on my heart. There is loss. There is fear. The sin against the Holy Spirit and my contempt flood my mind. I have fear that presses me against a wall. I keep walking and the glitter and shadow are gone. I am left with a split mind. My thoughts are jumbled. The bubbles did this. My mind can't stop. I sit down and look at my wrist. I see a scar that I have always had. It isn't a cut or a birthmark. It is like strange chunks that form a line. The line means something. I will face hell and spit at the idea of hate. It's too much. What am I thinking? I have always had this mark.

I am sitting in my room now trying to get rid of my confusion. Maybe there is a reason for it. I can remember my Mom telling me a story about when I was a child and I was sick. She was in the room with me and I started talking to someone. I told her not to worry, that the man said everything will be all right. She smiled at me and told me to enjoy my visit with Jesus. I hate this thing on my arm. I can't do this. I am not a miracle child. I am a freak. I can't live this life anymore. I won't be this. I am no teacher. They are all against me. They are all against me. I am no Superman as the words, false prophet, pull on my soul.

I look at the Coors brewery and I see a huge tower. I realize what I have to do. I have to stand on top of it and throw my garbage-wasted body onto the solid pavement. Go, and go as fast as you can. I will wear my Broncos shirt and let it wrap me in my death. I start walking fast and I think of Jayde. She needs me. My mind is still reeling and my confusion is in pace with my energy. I'm in a deep melancholic hole. I keep thinking about Hell and whether it exists. I think about my family. It hurts and I keep walking. I committed sin against the Holy Spirit, the one unforgivable sin. I did it. They all hate me and I just want to get rid of the poison.

I am going to get out of here. At last, freedom.

Everyone can see through me. I can never have peace. I pick up the phone and leave a message for my mom. "Mom, I know the truth and I will see you in the insane asylum." I pick up my guitar and throw it down. I pace around the room. I have so much energy and I realize I haven't slept or eaten anything in a while. I start watching TV and block out what they are saying and try to just stare. I pick up the Bible. I realize this sudden urge for Scripture is no good. The words keep changing. What are you doing, Toby? Like Alice from Alice in Wonderland, you can't find a white rabbit to help you. I keep following white because it feels right. I follow the white flashes. I follow the white to make myself good and clean again. But I am not clean, or perfect like a savior should be. I drive to my Mom's. She hasn't checked her messages, so I tell her what's going on. "There is still a part of me that is me," I tell her. She and my sister look at me in horror.

*Muttle*
*Muttle*
*Muttle*
*Muttle*

# 14

## Trying to Bury the Dream

I had been barking at my Mom that I had committed the sin against the Holy Spirit, the unforgivable sin. She told me that if I was so freaked out about it, there was no way I could have done it. My contempt, and the arrogance that made me stand so tall, was the reason for me committing the unforgivable sin. She talked me into going to see a therapist.

Everyone went to bed. I was alone. I started thinking about my dreams and I came to the realization that my biggest dream had been to play Red Rocks Amphitheater and tour the rest of my life playing music. The dream of playing at Red Rocks was over. My guitar felt wrong and I was sick of it. I was not proud of my playing. I could do covers all right but the album I made was not great. I couldn't see myself as a person who could stand on a stage in front of a bunch of people.

I decided to go to Red Rocks. I grabbed my guitar. The night was calling out my name and I was going to answer. My mind was in turmoil and I couldn't keep a straight thought. I started driving. I turned off the radio. I didn't feel like listening to the backwards talk. I made my way to Red Rocks and passed Mathews Winters, a trail where I had mountain biked so many times. That was until I got bitten by a rattlesnake. The snake popped out of the bushes and hit me on the back. It didn't puncture my skin but left me with a terrible rash.

I started up the winding road to Red Rocks and thought about all the shows I had seen there. I thought about Coalesce. I had watched the sun come up with her one morning.

I marched to the top of the stairs but my mind wasn't right. I wanted to play with no one around. *I will give my music dream to God after I finish playing tonight. No one will ever know.* I have this feeling that God isn't there for me anymore and that is a hell I can't live in. *If I stop playing guitar I give up the thing I love most in the world and maybe then I can connect with God again.* There has to be a reason I am so wrapped up in this religion stuff. I was the guy in college who left that behind me and lived for the moment, but now it had its grip on me, like a vice holding two pieces of wood. I want to play Red Rocks and then let my dreams go. My friends will ask me why I don't play guitar anymore, but I will be able to look back on this night and know I played my ass off and gave my art to Him. *I feel contempt for God and the only way for me to feel empowered is to give up my guitar. The words tumble in my head while I barter with God, but I figure he can appreciate it more than anyone because he can see my heart.*

I stand there staring at the dark stage, at the dark night. I am not scared of the dark. I am afraid of this sickness and the sickness sparks a dark 'muttle' in my head. It is a cloud of fear. It is a fear I have never known and with it comes a darkness that makes me run.

I make my way down the stairs where two raccoons fight in a trash can. I don't want to hear that sound. The rawness of it is so hard. I run down the stairs and put my guitar in the back of my car and drive back to my mom's house. The 'muttle' sticks with me as I pull into the driveway. Thankfully, everyone is asleep. I walk into the family room and pick up the Bible. I start reading a part in Jeremiah where many people have died. Suddenly, I find myself in the bathroom sitting in the corner and the darkness that is in my head is something I now can see. Not with my eyes, but it's there. Fear hits me and I know I can't do it. I realize that I am just hurting myself and whatever God is plaguing me with is probably in my own mind. The fear is clinging to me like duct tape. It is the true nature of the fear of God I have in me. I make my way into the tub and am in the fetal position but I can't escape the fear. I want to be dead. I want to roll up in a ball and disappear. I get out of the tub and I go back to the Bible and read about the sin against the Holy Spirit and then the words begin to speak -- to scream at me: Jesus will take care of this.

I drove to my apartment. When I got home I felt okay and the thoughts were settling down but I knew I could spin out of control at any moment. I was sick of it. I couldn't get rid of the prison I was in. I wanted to think clearly. I meditated to clear my thoughts. I sat in the middle of the room in complete silence while the meditation gave me a little comfort.

***

I had talked with my boss at the coffee shop after the day I didn't show up for work and told her I was having problems with my father's death and told her that I was sorry that I missed work. She was genuinely concerned and let me keep my job.      Somehow, I was getting to work. I didn't know how, but I was. Leaving work, one night after closing, I put on Johnny Cash and I felt sympathy. I felt sympathy for those left behind. Before I knew it I was listening to "Man in Black" and I could feel my brother singing with me. I could even hear his off-pitch voice. The song means so much to me and it cries out like a weeping river.

The days were rugged and I couldn't tell them apart. I went into each day not knowing how I got there. The fear calmed like the tide washing up on the beach. The desire to walk was stronger than anything I have ever known.

Walking, I tuned into a song that made me feel like I was in a cave. All I had was an ancient lighted torch. The fire represented the wisdom of the world. The torch was solid in my hand. At the end of the cave there was a garden full of life. In the garden I was free from myself. I was free from the world and its judgmental eyes. I was just me. The thought of this torch gave me hope that I would get through this.

I walked for about thirty minutes on a path parallel to Clear Creek. I looked over at some bushes and was amazed at what I saw. There was a three foot long torch on some bush. I couldn't believe it. I had the vision of my torch and somehow it had been placed there for me. It was a sign or an omen? Maybe it was a coincidence, but it felt like something was trying to connect with me. What was going on? What were the odds of this happening? What was I supposed to do with this sign? At the end of the torch was a glass ball that had been broken. Maybe this sign represented me and my own lack of wisdom. I left the torch and kept walking. I wondered what the torch meant and what I was supposed to do about it. Maybe it was God's way of telling me I will be all right. I walked home and was plagued by what this meant. I slept well on this night.

The next day passed quickly. I had this feeling that I was going to be struck by something and my hair would turn white. It seemed logical. Was it something I read in the Bible? It felt like the white would scar my face too. Will it happen?

*Muttle*
*Muttle*
*Muttle*
*Muttle*

# 15

## Here come the machines

It had been a month since my father had died and I was feeling like half a man. I turned on the news and saw that there was a forest fire raging between Golden and Boulder. I had to see the heart of the fire. I got in my car and started driving. I pictured firemen with giant hoses trying to overcome the beast in my mind. I drove fast. I could see the fire in the distance and it was huge. The smoke looked like it came from a volcano. I followed a windy road that led to it and there standing in a yard were a bunch of people. They were just looking at the smoke and talking to each other. I left my car and stood with these people for a few minutes.

*Go into the forest. I have to go into the forest. I have to go toward the fire.*

I leapt out of the yard and started running toward the plume of smoke. I could hear people muttering behind me. The fire was getting closer and burned out of control. If I got too close to the fire it could turn on me but I had to see the heart of the fire. All I could see now was smoke.

*Touch the fire.*

I got closer and closer until close was too close.

*Carry a rock up the mountain for all the soldiers who have died. Not just our American soldiers but all soldiers.*

I picked up a giant rock. Suddenly, there was an explosion close to me. I didn't drop my stone. I turned away from the heart of the fire and started climbing as high as I could go. There wasn't a trail so I had to make one for myself.

*The fire wants me to save the stone. I need to get it up the mountain.*

I continued climbing until I reached the top. There was a small ledge and I placed the rock on the ledge.

*The fire will not disturb it.*

As I walked down the mountain, dodging the fire and the fire fighters, I knew intimately the fear of the elements. I knew that some people would call this little expedition stupid but I felt wonderful because I had seen something out of control. I was out of control and now I knew that there were other things on this earth that were out of control.

\*\*\*

The next day I made an appointment with a therapist. I needed help.

I drove around counting white cars and white signs. I passed Alex on the street. Alex has an open mind. He reminds me of me. We talk about religion and he talks about being a pagan. He doesn't exactly say that he is a pagan but says he understands it more because loving a pagan is something Christians don't do.

*Loving the so called enemies is the truth about Jesus. That is the idea of Christianity.*

We decided to go to Burger King. Our religious discussion goes on and he talks about who he believes in, and points to a tree and calls it the tree of life.

*He insinuates that he will kill me in the third year.*

I wonder, "Will he kill me when I am thirty?" The

fear of him doing this makes me uneasy. The conversation continues but I don't hear what he says.

We made our way back into Golden and I headed home. I needed a new tape recorder to help me with my songs so I headed for the basement. I found myself standing at the top of the stairs with a feeling of falling. I looked down the stairs and the simple act of putting one foot in front of the other paralyzed me. It was like there were no stairs and if I took a step I'd fall. The feeling was so strong that I retreated to my room.

I felt so good when I was hanging out with a friend and not thinking about my sick brain. Screw ecstasy----- it's like poison. I was in my room and the same trapped feeling came over me. I was locked in a jail. I laid on my bed in the middle of the day and I saw an image of Jesus on the cross. He was on the other side of the wall and His right fist was huge. There was anger in this hallucination or delusion or vision. He was only a machine. He wasn't there, but I pressed against the bed hoping that it would go away. The figure was huge. I had to open the door. I had to face it. This was my first encounter with the machines. I could see on the other side of the door and I pushed open the door like a child opening the closet door to see if a monster was in there. I saw nothing. I walked to the same steps and I reached my foot out to the step below and felt that it was solid. I started laughing. It felt good. Almost like me. All I could do was laugh.

I drove to Soundtrack to buy a tape recorder and on my way back to my car it happened again. I was standing five feet from my car, touching the ground with my toe before I took a step and I again felt genuine fear.

I started driving and lost myself. Where did I just go? Oh yeah, I look at the device next to me and realize where I was. Thousands of thoughts were muttering around and I forgot all the basic functions of day to day life. I still followed white everywhere.

I decided to go for a walk. Walking was my only release because if my feet walked faster than my brain could think, then I could almost make sense of my thoughts. I decided to make a trek up Table Mountain. I had to conquer the mountain that made me this way and I can't let these machines take over my brain.

As I stood at the trailhead, I saw the most amazing dog I have ever seen. It was a white lab, and I wanted it. No one would know. It was so beautiful. I checked his tags and the address on the tag was only a few blocks away. I started following this white creature up the hill. He marked his territory every fifteen feet. Today was a good day and I was not going to follow white symbols anymore, I was going to follow the white dog. We trekked around the mountain and made our way to the top. I felt like Adam, the first man. We were alone as night fell.

The walk was long and I sat with the animal and we drank water that had pooled on a rock. We made our way down the mountain and I took the dog to his owners.

I made my way back to the apartment and sat in front of the TV. A woman from Haiti was on and she was talking about how all you have to do is pray and God will release you from your burden. I started praying with her. She was passionate in her beliefs and I prayed for release from the sickness.

*Muttle*

*Muttle*

*Muttle*

*Muttle*

# 16

## The Silver Creature

I waited in the lounge of the therapist's office and gazed at magazines plastered with faces of pretty people living perfect lives. Children are raised to worship these beautiful creatures. Suddenly I went from being a man who was jealous of these people to a man who saw the nature of man and felt that they were no better than me. I felt it in my bones.

Dr. Gilbert was an older man with white hair and a rather solemn look. He called me in and immediately I felt threatened by him. *The bad energy is on his side and it is against me. I can see it in his eyes when he lowers his glasses and questions my motives.* We talk and I feel the desire to be honest with him. If only I can be honest with one person. I dive into the mixing bowl of my truth even though I see the bad energy. People tell me that I can trust a therapist and so I try. I tell him that I have committed the sin against the Holy Spirit. He sort of laughs and tells me that if I am afraid I have done it then I haven't done it. He doesn't understand my arrogance, my blasphemy and feeling like a savior ready to save the world from it callousness.

He asks about my past. I tell him about my father and even tell him about my contempt with God. There is no reaction from him. He sits with his glasses perched on his nose and acts like he has the great answer, but it is hidden in a box locked away forever. I then tell him that my contempt has made me into something I am not. He asks me why I feel that way. I tell him that I turned my back on God and He has forsaken me.

"It's weird though, Dr. Gilbert, even though God is against me, I still see drops of heaven and whispers of redemption. When I go for my walks sometimes I see things the same way that I saw things when I was okay. Sometimes I see things that are so beautiful that they make my eyes well up. What does that mean?"

"Well, son, what does it mean to you?"

In my head I am thinking: "I asked you a question and I need a fucking answer not a therapist's, side stepping, dribble." I sit across from this old man like there is a chess board between us. What move is he going to make?

He then asks about my job. I am spent on answering from the honesty bowl. I tell him my dribble about work. Not one thing is accomplished except that he tells me to set goals for myself. He speaks like the Word of God is coming from his mouth. I think his knight just took my pawn.

He says something about Sudan. *I can't believe it. Did he just say Sudan? It is a sign. It is a piece of the puzzle.*

* * *

I went straight to a grocery store after my session. I was still following white and was trying to laugh about it. I bought a map of the United States. I saw that Golden was in the middle of the country and realized that if I compare it to a map of the world, it looks just like Israel and the Muslim Nations at the center.

*I try to figure out how to get to Sudan and after doing all the mathematics I see a city that corresponds to it. That is where I need to go. I will just get in my car and drive.*

*I went to the park. I pulled on the latch that led to the park. I chain-smoked to calm myself. I picture people and I can feel their energy or lack thereof. When I smoke it feels like they are dying. I keep smoking to make it better. I can't stop smoking because it is the one thing I have that makes me feel good, and then I realize this thinking is deluded. I keep smoking and burning people down. I think about the reality of it. But I can feel the act of burning so strongly. It's coming from an outside source, not from my head. I am in hell and don't know how to get out. I am killing by smoking, and saving, by softly blowing. I think of actors and their arrogance. I think of musicians and their arrogance and I am burning them down with each puff. I then see arrogance in the people that come into my coffee shop.*

*Burn Suzie down.*

*Burn Paul down.*

*Burn everyone down.*

That night as I sit in the park I am glad I don't have the Bible in hand. I can't understand the Bible anymore so why listen to the screaming. I keep hurting myself. This morning I burned my foot with a cigarette. It felt so good. The pain was what I needed at that moment. I know it will leave a scar but I feel like I need a good scar right now. Karlee was going into work right after I burned myself. It was four o'clock in the morning and I had been out all night. She had a look of fear on her face. She doesn't know I'm harmless. Except to myself.

A couple days later I hurt myself again. I wanted to see my blood. I wanted to see it dripping. I went to a secluded spot and found a strong piece of wood-- a two by four. I started punching it. I had to make my fists solid and square. I kept punching this thing and suddenly my fists were bruised. There was no stream of red, only a dull ache. I kept punching. Finally, after beating the thing over and over, the blood made its way onto the ground. It was dripping red.

It made a four inch pool of pure blood across the board. My hand was bruised and I thought it might be broken. When that didn't appease my desire for pain, I decided to give myself a tattoo. The needle was too dull and it left me with a sore ankle.

I still wasn't appeased. Kelly was gone when I got back to the apartment. I thought of the Islam nation and suddenly an idea. I (the arrogant fuck that I am) wanted to guarantee heaven for them. I went to the shelf and found a huge jug of vinegar. I opened it and started chugging. I drank it all and immediately went to the toilet and the vomit spewed.

I went out walking. With head phones on I walked through Golden.

*I see Alex riding a surf board, which is floating and moving fast, against specks in the air. He is riding on the music in my ear. For a moment, he is my hero. I know he has been wronged in his life and I want to see the kid "shine." I see all the people I care about on the surf board. They are my heroes. They are all heroes doing the impossible. The picture is vivid. So real I wonder if I'm hallucinating. I think of all the Armageddon stuff that is preached and before I know it, there in front of me, a giant silver creature starts killing people on the surf board with a spear. The giant silver creature is justified because he can see the heart of man. I look at him hoping I will be next, because I have grown tired.*

This vision is too much to handle. I sprint down the streets of Golden.

*Get the chemicals out.*

*I keep running until my knee starts hurting. I have a huge screw that goes through my entire leg below my left knee -- an old sports injury. Is my father is trying to punish me for being a failure? Am I the giant silver creature?*

*Muttle*

*Muttle*

*Muttle*

*Muttle*

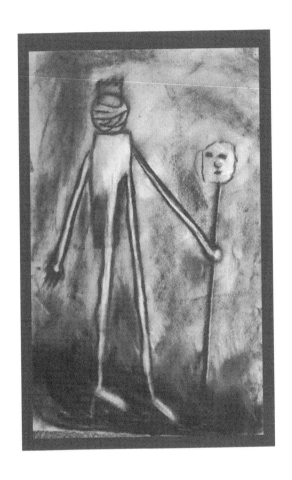

# 17

## The Gypsy

I feel so much better. A rich day sounds its horn and I am inspired to give what I can. I head over to my Mom's house. It feels like the tires are lifting the car as I drive. It feels like there are four beings; one on each wheel. It is so real but is it a figment of my imagination? I feel like I have done something wrong to the family and I am looking for release. My Mom is at work. I see my sister in the kitchen and her eyes, her eyes, they are a red scream. Her eyes are open and sad. Fire and anger are there. Her pressure pushes against me. I can see her eyes look at me, but it isn't her eyes. My sister blurts out something and it's so much louder than it should be. There is anger in her voice. I can't be with my sister.

I sit with Jayde for a while and she has this weird toy that makes marbles keep going with no end or beginning. It represents to me the nature of God. Spheres keep dropping and falling. But I know that someone put the first marble in the machine!! I decide to go home and give Jayde a kiss goodbye.

I start driving home and the wheel thing with my car is not there, thank God! I keep going until I get to my apartment. I have to get some groceries. There is a song that has an Iggy Pop sort of sound and I suddenly have the idea that I'm going to take down the system. It is raw and reckless. There is a calm arrogance to me as I listen to the song. My arrogance continues.

On my way to the grocery store I saw the guy who was in the coffee shop filling out an application a couple weeks earlier. He looks exactly like the European version of Jesus. When he was in the shop he stuttered so severely that you could barely understand him. I notice his face, like stone, and he is walking straight with his head up. It's amazing to see a piece of rock walking. For a second I wonder if it is Jesus, alive, here to fulfill the prophecies. I want to talk to him. If he isn't here to save the world then maybe I can help this kid out. I circle the block but I can't find him. I drive away in a state of unrest. I'm so sick of judging and letting all my theories burn holes in my brain. I am an intelligent man. How did I find this circle of madness? I go home and I grab a bunch of money and drive as fast as I can downtown. I see a bum on the street and he looks like he is waiting for me. He is in my head reading my mind just like everyone else is in my head. I want to help the world. He is black and wears glasses. It was nice out but I assumed he was still wearing heavy clothing from the cold night before. I was parked close to him and I got out of my car and gave him the money. I walked away fast because I didn't want him to see my face. I heard in the background the man saying, "Thank you, I can sleep in a hotel for a while." I got into my car and I drove. I think of him in a hotel and my eyes start to glass over. Analyzing it, I think, "Maybe I did it to feel better, maybe I am a self righteous prick but in my selfish way it feels good to know he will be in a hotel." As I drive I have so much energy that I feel confined in the space I am in. I wish

I could do more than just hand out fists-full of money.

I had to work for the next few days, going in at 4 O'clock in the morning to open. I watched the sun come up through the window of the coffee shop. The bad energy I had felt the last few days turned into bliss. I was at peace. Then the people started coming in. *Every person has sad eyes. It looks like every customer has been crying. It feels like they know something I don't. Their eyes are wide and I feel like telling the people to leave me alone. I'm not afraid to speak to them but I somehow know that they can't control their eyes. For three days I see nothing but sad, red eyes.*

The days ran into each other and I couldn't tell one from the next. I had to look at the calendar to figure out when I worked next. This was difficult because I didn't have any concept of when I had worked last or whether I worked open or closes or what. I asked my roommate constantly what day it was.

Diana seemed to come in every day and she brought warmth with her that got me through the day. She was the only one who made sense when she talked. I liked her but I couldn't tell if she was there to help me or if she was there because I was supposed to connect with her. My mind was still rolling on two avenues but the avenues randomly merged. One of those nights when I got off work, I nestled in the park and dreamt of being with her. I liked the dream. When I was younger I used to pray for my future wife. I thought that God had her all picked out for me and I would pray that wherever she lived, that she was good and happy. It was a child's prayer. I am drawn to the idea that destiny is the path chosen and there is purpose in it. If you take a clock and break it all apart, put it in a can and shake it for a hundred years or a thousand years, the pieces would still be just pieces. They would never be a clock. There has to be a hand to put the pieces together in order for the clock to be a clock again. I let words like destiny echo in me.

Where is my free will?

*I am controlled by the machines as my mind drives down*

*two lanes like two cars in a race.*
*Muttle*
*Muttle*
*Muttle*
*Muttle*

A girl that I have never seen comes into the coffee shop and when she talks her words cover me with tinsel. We are connected. She has sharp features and is pretty. She has a tattoo on her arm that shows her style and we connect with our speech. She has long straight blond hair and she has a long thin body. She wears clothes with a dab of rebellion. Her aura screams, "I'm unique. I'm different." Now somewhere in my subconscious I laugh at her being with me, but there is some internal force and there are outside energies that are pulling me. She tells me about how she went to France for a semester and she traveled all of Europe. She also traveled when she was younger because her father was in the Armed Forces. I tell her she is a gypsy and she just laughs. The words are like fire in the air and she is proud of the name I give her. This girl is connected to something. The places she has been and the things she has seen are incredible. There are other energies that I feel that stem from different things and I am intrigued by it but I realize I am probably going crazy. I think of a pagan Wiccan goddess and it satisfies my stillness. I can't tell if her eyes are blue or green but they shine so much I have to look away. As she leaves me, she insinuates something big is going to happen but this only comes from a backward look from her wicked eyes. This would be the last time I would see her at the coffee shop.

I punch out on the time clock and walk home. As I walk I pass the "Amsterdam" looking apartments, the one with the tiny beach across Clear Creek. I can see her going into them. Did I see her or is this just something that I am imagining? The gypsy feels close and I am surprised and psyched that she lives here. A light turns on in an apartment room and I assume it is hers. I think of her and Diana. Two girls magnified.

Walking home, I think about my friends and how disconnected I am from them. I am alone out here on the streets of Golden. I find little patches of heaven everywhere I go, followed with dread. I find signs and omens everywhere. Heaven has golden streets. That is a sign. Maybe heaven is on earth. Maybe heaven will show itself to me again if God wants it to. Maybe one day when someone figures it out, the puzzle and the little patches of heaven will all be one piece like a quilt. Am I supposed to figure it out? Maybe there are people out there who each have a piece of the puzzle and once they get together true peace will come. If only people could see what I see and feel what I feel-- the highs, the lows.

I keep smoking people down. I can't help it. Cigarettes are all I have. I smoke them down and then I smoke them up. It leaves a bad taste in my mouth, to kill someone when you don't want to. I finally realize I have no power and only God can judge these people.

The gypsy's words from our meeting echo and ring like bells in my subconscious. She is reaching out to me. The word pagan gypsy hits me hard. I feel like she has power. I am on some crazy trip and it is all connected. I walk around town between buildings. Suddenly, I see strange lights in everything. I see them mostly in the plants and trees. The gypsy is talking to me. It is her? I feel an energy outside myself that is her. Maybe God is giving me little spots of joy in every step I take. She follows me, so I follow her. I feel good today and I am going to wander around until I stop seeing the gypsy. An hour passes and the night comes and maybe I will dream of her tonight.

Work again. I better get there! No, I don't have to work today. Do I or don't I? I don't know. Oh well, if I have to work they will call me. Kelly is gone for the day and I am caught up in my self absorbed state and I don't want it to end. There is this energy outside myself that is almost like a conversation. Someone is talking to me and telling me where to go. I think of the gypsy and how I could win her over or maybe the sweet girl, Diana. I could be with her. Which one? I'm a lonely soul and I feel like I don't have anyone but I feel like there are too many people around me. I start marching down to the little sand pit where I see the gypsy's window. It is dark out. I have my harmonica handy and I find myself tasting melodies. I can feel the gypsy's window from the energy outside myself. I sit with my feet in the sand and a large rock behind me. I play my harmonica like oversized wind. I need to practice more but how can I concentrate for that long. I can concentrate now. I feel like she isn't there so I get up and start walking back home. I take my shirt off because I am the kind of guy that doesn't like to wear clothing unless I have to. All of a sudden my dick gets hard. It is so hard that it hurts. The pain is swelling and I can't figure it out. I wonder if it is the gypsy that is doing some witchcraft because the pressure is getting tighter. The pain is so strong and I can't stop it. I put my shirt on and walk down to the tiny beach. In my mind I say I am sorry for the arrogance and suddenly the pushing stops. I am fucked up at this point because I can't figure out if it is my subconscious or some strange voodoo. It came from nowhere. I walk back to my apartment and there is my bed. I lay down and a smell comes out of nowhere. It is so sweet I can't believe it. It is the best smelling thing I have ever smelled. I lay down and the energy around me starts messing with me again. The energies are all over the place. It feels good but it feels disgusting at the same time. It is like machines all around me making everything grope me. It finally stops and I am sitting on my bed wondering what it was. I was tired and I couldn't remember the last time I had eaten. I put my head on the pillow and slept.

The next day I woke up and the day before was like some kind of dream. I seemed to have fallen into some strange state of trying to figure out puzzles, and absorbing everything I could. I was driving, just to drive, and dancing around my head was the idea of chariots. The Bible says in the last days there will be chariots and I think about the cars we drive. Wait, maybe I made up the chariot thing a few mornings ago. I lay down and close my eyes. In my head a hand is reaching across to hold mine on the other side of the garden. The picture is sublime and there is so much connection in it. What or who is reaching out to me? I think it might be Christ. If only I could find one person that understands.

There is a picture that gets stuck in my head. It is a picture of me with my Broncos shirt on with boxing gloves. Opposite me, my brother stands with dark clothes on like Johnny Cash's "Man in Black." I remember, he told me about a murder case where the families of the victim shook him up. Suddenly, I am on the victim's side and he is on the murderer's side. I am punching him, and he is punching me. We seem to be fighting over the justice of the victims or a second chance -- forgiveness for the murderer. It feels like a fight with sparks. It's so real. Then he and I change places and I am in his shoes and he is in mine. I am still wearing my Broncos shirt and he is still in dark clothing. This fight goes on for a while and a feeling of frustration starts to get to me. I am sick of these pictures. They won't go away. I put an angry song on and the desire to fight hits me. I just want something real. I cut a tattoo on the bottom of my foot in the shape of an hourglass. Now that was real.

My brother comes to visit me in Golden and we make our way to the railroad tracks by my house. We are standing on the tracks and I see us fighting. I want to feel something real again. I see him hitting me, and realize that is something he would never do. I can see in the world the anger that leads to no mercy and I don't want to feel that kind of anger. I finally get the nerve to tell him about what is going on with me. He tells me to put it in a box and throw it away. The walk on the tracks is nice. There are several trains. How I wish to just get out of town and find a place where the darkness doesn't lie. I told him about the torch and he brushed it off like it was just a strange coincidence. We kept talking and he tells me he is going to visit mom, my sister and Jayde. We go our separate ways.

The night began and I was ready to go. I put on my hoodie and listened to some music. There are no white dogs to follow. They are only in my mind. I am sitting on the pavement steps and I laugh at the fact that my brother has the anarchy tattoo on his ass. I think about the world. Everyone I know is in a tribe. Some people are alone like I am tonight but I have all sorts of tribes that I am in; Lisa and Zane, Caleb and Andrea, Karlee and Kelly and my family. There are tribes on the streets. There are tribes in office buildings. There are tribes of friends that talk. There are tribes of police. There are tribes in government. There are small subcultures that individuals connect with. There are tribes in churches.

Muttle

Muttle

Muttle

Tonight is strange. I can't shake this religious stuff so why not just go with it. I am sitting in the park and I am digging.

Muttle
Muttle
Muttle

I wonder why I am here. I am still a child. I was not supposed to be here. All the years my parents spent together and doctors said there is a one in a million chance. Maybe I am some strange freak meant to dance with all the freaks. Maybe I am here to stop people from calling people freaks. I am definitely in hell but I also see heaven on earth. My little tidbits of knowledge are God's way of saying, "Its okay and someday the heaven that men hope for will be revealed." Is that the reason I am here? Am I supposed to look for heaven? It is hurting me to have to do it. I have grown to love the ups and downs but the delusions have taken me places I should not go. I still love it.

I wander around in the park and try to think of every sin known to man and I try to be that sin.

I sit in the grass and I think of a rapist. I start digging and imagine what a rapist must think. If there is some joy in raping someone, open your fucking eyes and understand that there can be no joy in the actual act. The only pleasure that rapist could possibly have is the joy of having power over someone. Power is nothing more than a delusion; a delusion that Mr. CEO lives in.

I then think of a murderer and there are so many elements to it. Cold blooded murder is nothing more than showing no mercy and feeling that the power to overtake someone is more important than life itself. Power is in a man's fist and when his heart is twisted, he wants to exert his power so he uses fists, like monsters, to murder. A fist can be creative too. A fist that makes sculptures is life because it brings something good in the world. Fists bring art and music and there is a wholesome power to that.

I then think of marriage and I start walking. I look

at two separate trees that are defined in two different ways each one casts a different shadow. They sit beside each other in peace. I start getting pissed off because I have been through my parents' divorce shit and all I saw in it was selfishness. If you get married and take the vows and don't live by them you have compromised yourself. But there is always forgiveness. I feel strong about this because I think there was a good chance for my parents to stay together. If there had been remorse for the infidelity, there could have been forgiveness. I think of my sister and her husband getting divorced after being married for three years. I watch little Jayde going back and forth every week. It affects her in more ways than the courts and the parents could imagine. What about Jayde? I mean no offense to my sister, but no one hears Jayde's voice. It seems to be only a tug of war between two sides. If you choose to divorce, one person should take custody and the other person should stand still. Parents want their rights but don't care about the kids' rights. Then I think of our government. YOU! Politicians. Judges. Open your fucking eyes! There is so much power in what you do.

I walk around thinking about sin all night. I think it will be the end of my journey. Maybe, if I find the right answers, all this struggling will be over and I will die. The martyr no one knows. Screw this martyr shit. I'm so selfish that I couldn't be a martyr.

When I finish wandering around trying to save myself and the world, I realize I still have to keep digging. I am not here to fulfill any great thing and my friends have their own conscience and it isn't for me to judge. I have to stop judging people and start judging ideas: (I always loved that philosophy.) Truth is out there only because I can feel it when I touch my face. Does that mean I know the truth? No, but the wheels in my head are rolling toward it even if I don't want to know it. The delusions have led me to stare into the abyss and look for gold. The delusions have led me to this state of being completely self absorbed and I can't stop. I am just a delusional freak. But maybe it's all true and I will flow out of the abyss. I need help but I can't talk to the shrink.

It's blasphemy I am speaking and feeling. The word "ego" is screaming at me on the way to my apartment. Tonight I will put one full bottle of pills next to my bed. Maybe during the night I will kill myself. If only I had the courage. I lay in bed and I feel a fever and my heart hurts. There is a sharp pain in the front of my chest. I say, "Toby, it is just anxiety. Grandpa Tolini and father both died of a heart attack and maybe all the drugs I've done will kill me." Suddenly the smell comes again and it comforts me.

The next day I drive to a hardware store to get some paint. I have to paint the dreariness of my room. I meet Alex while listening to Bob Dylan. He and I decide to walk the tracks.

Muttle

Muttle

Muttle

Muttle

We start talking and I tell him that one day he might have to kill me and he knows I am insane. So we keep talking and he tells me that I have gotten arrogant. He says to get off my cross. The words ring and I realize that I am wandering around lost in nonsense. Now the wheels on the machines are turning so fast in my head and I am scared that they might never go away.

I had to go get the paint. I left Alex and headed to the store. I was standing waiting for my paint to be mixed. There were a few people around and I felt such a freedom. My friend, Leah, is a dancer and she taught me some tap dancing at a party. I found myself in the hardware store dancing my ass off. People looked at me like they would look at a car wreck and that made it even funnier. I didn't stop and people got so uncomfortable that they looked away from me. I kept doing it because it was fun. I wanted to do my

Charlie Chaplin impersonation but I didn't have my cane. When my paint was mixed, my feet stopped moving. It wasn't funny. Those people like to watch a clown. I'm not a clown. I can feel the way they are looking at me. They think I'm an abomination. What am I? This entire scene is just too funny.

# 18

## The Gypsy Calls

After speeding home I see the poison. I find the apartment empty.

I think of the gypsy and I want to meet her under her apartment window. I can feel her so strongly it almost makes my bones shake. There is a sickness that comes with yearning for something beautiful. It is yearning to not be alone. I stand under her window waiting for a sign and one is given to me. I look at her window and I can feel her with someone else. It makes me sick. I wonder if it is the poison. I stand there and wonder why she called me. Why does the energy call me? Is she just another machine calling my name? Is she even behind that window? Maybe I called her. Maybe I am standing on my little beach totally delusional. The jealousy of her being with another man makes me sick. My stomach hurts and I am so depressed. But she is still there with me. She seems to have a longing to be with someone and maybe that person is with her now and she is in his arms. I start to walk away and she puts her head out of the window and I feel her screaming at me. The energy is screaming at me. I can feel her screams like the tearing of my flesh. Another dark machine starts screaming at me too. It is coming from a different window and it feels like it could be a machine too. His anger is so strong that he starts punching me. At this point I have nothing left to do but laugh and shriek at these imaginary beings that are outside of me. There is a perversion that is coming through the gypsy's window and I don't want it. Maybe I don't want her. The feeling is frustration. I can't take it. She is calling out to me but only in imaginary rage. The perversion makes me almost curious -- like a man would be in a land of sirens; I suppose any man would wonder what was going on behind those closed windows. I try to shake the perversion off my shoulders but it won't go away. It is sticking like pigeon feathers to tar. I dig deeper and the machines are trying to crush me into a place where blood and flesh cannot be. I start walking away because the mania kicks in and I don't want the perversion. I just need answers and have no clue where to find them. A dull cord pulls me down to aloneness. I am alone.

I take a long stretch up the stream. I want to go and not stop, just feel my legs moving with the waves crashing behind me. I find the spot. It is the spot where the light from the creek ends and runs upstream. It is almost completely covered by the trees and blackness. I know it is a long trek down the dark path at the end of Clear Creek and my shadow scares me. The trees are playing tricks with me and the shadows of the leaves dance. I find myself in a state of fear walking into the blackness but I have to find the end. I keep walking and I am listening to music but the music can't hide the darkness. So will the darkness and I meet and shake hands or will I live with it as my plague? Will it consume me? I keep walking and I am there, I am at the end of the dirt road. I have smoked cigarettes from there to here. I realize I have to walk back. The idea of walking back is terrifying but I turn around. The walk back into the light is harder than the walk into the darkness. There are so many shapes and shadows and things to make me look back. As I make it into the light the shadows haven't gone away. So I just keep going.

Where two streets cross there are no twigs. There is only one twisted man. The cross street sits like a well; no bottom to the well. I stand in the middle. I look in all directions and the streets seem to stretch in crooked crazy patterns. I wonder if, like the old great blues players, I will sell my soul. I have come to a place where the straight path collides with the reckless path. Maybe I will sell my soul, make a ton of money and give the majority of it to the poor. Wait, can you sell your soul and help people? I wonder. I wonder if I could touch heaven through the streets. I will sell my soul to get out of this place and give to the poor. I take my cigarette and put it out on the middle of the street. I realize I have crossed a line and cut God. A panic hits me and a rolling in my head starts. Am I mad? I immediately jump in my car and have nowhere to go. I have turned my back on God. He has turned His back on me. I lost myself. I have lost myself. The child that loves is now a maniac. I start driving and decide to drive up Lookout Mountain. The road twists around and around. It goes this way and that way and I have to be alert.

It is about 2 or 3 O'clock in the morning and my anger toward myself makes me take the tiny curves like a maniac. I am driving fast around the turns because I don't care if I fly off the mountain. I always wanted to fly and a car would suit me just fine for transportation. I am listening to a singer that makes me want to drive off the road and see where I land. I get to the top and turn my car around. The drive down is different. I am glued to the lights from the city. They are cascading wonderment. It is calm. I realize that I am foolish and I don't think God would hold it against me if I have truly sold my soul. It is amazing what desperation brings. He can see the sickness inside of me. I keep driving

and driving and driving.
Muttle
Muttle
Muttle

    I have to take control of this. Could medicine help? Forget that! I can control my brain myself. I will use meditation. I have to be calm. I sit in my room once I am home and I try to stop my brain from running. It doesn't work. My frustration is building and I am tired of the spinning. I am just tired. I look at my fan and suddenly it shows me something. Everything stretches out from me on the left side of the room and it looks like it is fifteen feet away. The right side to the window looks normal. It feels like a hole into some other dimension. How could the room stretch out like this? Would it be possible to visit that other dimension? It is so amazing, my arm reaches out to touch through it. I can only feel air. It is calling me. My father is telling me something. I can't understand him. I can sit here until I understand. Maybe he wants me to be with him on the other side. I stare at the fan for a while and decide to go to the living room. I am in awe of seeing what I have seen. I know in the Bible it says men will see visions. Well, I truly believe I have seen one now.

I pick up the guitar and I can't play. My fingers can't hold the guitar. I used to be so passionate about the guitar and now I have replaced the guitar with walking. There's truth out there, I know it. I am driven to wander and keep my eyes open.

I wander and then I return to my apartment. I go to sleep with the most wonderful smell filling me. Where is it coming from? It smells so good. I'll just sleep and remember the tastes God is giving me.

# 19

## Shiny Anger

I am awake. I see my brother and a big movie star sitting like brothers on a beach that is getting smaller and smaller. It is a dark place but it shines of men wasting away. What was that? I am immediately pissed off. The void.

The whole day is bad. Contempt is in me and it is making me smile. I can't control my smiles. They force themselves on me. I (contempt) smile during the day. I was working with Lisa and I wondered about her. She was all about the coffee shop. I thought, what was up with that? I knew she wasn't happy. I hoped someday she would find a job that could make her content. This day she was just intent.

A woman came in and asked for her "usual latte," I forgot what her "usual latte" was and looked up at her as I began to mark the cup. She looked at me or through me and slowly in the most disrespectful and condescending way said, "I want my usual: a 16 oz., 160 degree, non-fat, mocha with no whip latte." She was the customer and I was her slave.

I thought about how we are industrial slaves. I cleaned up crap when someone decided to rub it everywhere and I was totally bound to the job by the necessity of having to live with a roof over my head and heat and electricity and food, etc... I was still mopping the floors and trying to do it so it would bring glory to God.

My shift was over and I drove home. A natural high was with me, it was always with me.

The gypsy is plaguing me today and I see her like I see my brother, who seems to have a perfect life. My brother worked for it so why the jealousy? The gypsy is with my brother and it makes me sick. I can feel a presence connecting me to another energy, the energy of the other side. I have turned into a pagan and it doesn't feel right in my gut.

I love Julie (one of my Wiccan friends). The spiritual conversations with her ring in my brain. I am just too messed up. I wish I could have one clean and clear thought. Should a man feel like this? I pick apart religions and take something from each of them. Each one seems to be solid in its truth.

I am following the white again. I have to follow it now. I follow white cars for ten miles and end up laughing hysterically. What are you doing? That white lab was my dog and I should have kept it.

Muttle

Muttle

Muttle

I can't get the poison out of my head. Maybe some people know what I am thinking, while others don't. That lady today with the latte sure didn't act like she knew my thoughts. Some people just look at me and see right through me. I hate it. They know what I am thinking which makes me paranoid at what I am thinking.

I am sad. For one instant I feel connected to my father and then it is gone. I start walking up the creek and I walk to the sand pit and sit down on my rock. This is as close as I get to a beach. Maybe she (the gypsy) is looking down at me. She is just a bully like the rest of them. I am going to keep walking down the path. I see the Native American Statue and it always makes me smile. The statue has seen it all with me somehow. I guess there is a freedom about her and yet she has seen it all. I walk across the street. I am not dealing with the gypsy today and she isn't there anymore anyway. I think I will go to the big park and walk around in circles. Why the fuck not?

Muttle

Muttle

Muttle

I'm in my apartment and the up keeps going up. I am steaming and angry. That lady today was so condescending. I start thinking about all the kids who feel like crap because of someone's abuse.

That guy talking shit.

The guys at school that make people feel bad and the girls at school that do the same.

I guess everyone is trying to be their best. My own arrogance.

The best

The best

The best

The best

Muttle

The best

The best

The best

The best

Muttle

Tonight is the night! I am going to have a talk with the best and I am going to shake hands with the ground. I grab my MP3 player and start walking. I find the perfect CD, one that will shake the ground with me.

Muttle

I make the same trip down the dark walkway as I

did before. There is still blackness but I pass through the dark, talking back to the shadow leaves when they scream at me. I have to face my fears. I walk through the trees that echo fear and I am ready to face them. I think of Lisa who is so kind and I imagine her apartment and her posters of Ani Difranco and Janis Joplin. I think of the cuts she puts on her arm when she doesn't like herself. I think of my sister who has the same cuts on her arms. I think of my old college roommate. He was so cool before I saw him be abusive to the fat girl. We would talk about interesting things. I still see him doing push ups for hours. Why do people have to feel bad about themselves? Because they don't fit a mold? I can see all the actors and rock stars and one-hit wonders. Are these the things I want to be apart of? I can see all the senators, cops, magazines -- the magazines with their pristine pictures of beautiful people.

I think of the heavy-set girl who was in my dorm room and my roommate told her to get out because she was fat.

And so, I stand at the end of the dirt road facing pitch black. The only thing that faces me is trees. I look behind me and see the same dark road that I saw the other night.

I flick my sandals off behind me and then look at the wall of trees. There is anger with me but I am here to do a dance; a dance for anyone who can hear my feet, a dance because of the magazines. I think of my brother who was a boxer and how I used to hit his heavy bag as a kid. I think of how much he loves Muhammad Ali and how I wish I had the nerve to step into a real ring. I have my hood on as usual and I take it off. The night is cold but I know in a few moments that I will be sweating. This shadowbox is for the weak.

Muttle

Muttle

Muttle

Muttle

The steps I take are hard and I jump around.

My arms wave in the air and each swing feels like it makes contact.

I think about how Muhammad Ali would step and I try to make my steps count. I try to dance like he did when he boxed.

Faces pop up like popcorn.

I don't want to hurt anyone but just end the poverty and the downtrodden man.

I hope I don't hurt anyone with my mixing bowl of anger and the possibility of what is real.

Every country kills their people.

I see the government and corporate offices.

I see my face pop up and how thick my hypocrisy is and I swing at it.

I keep swinging.

I keep swinging.

Punch through it.

Faces keep popping up and I bring them down with swift blows. The power will always be in this world and I punch through it.

I think of my sister.

I think of Lisa.

I think of Lisa's mom telling her she should wear makeup.

I think of high school girls trying to fit in.

I think of high school jocks that hurt anyone who doesn't fit their mold. I think of the stoner crowd that pushes just as hard.

I think of me being the quarterback and walking around with arrogance flowing like a fountain.

Toby, you hypocrite!

Toby, you are a hypocrite!

My feet hurt against the ground, the tiny rocks.

There are no faces but I keep swinging, just keep going.

Hit the ground with your feet.
The tendon on the top of my ankle is hurting.
Keep going.
Keep going.

You're lost, Toby!
You're lost, Toby!
You're lost, Toby!
No more anger!
No more anger!
I realize how messed up I am.
You're lost, Toby!
You're lost, Toby!
I am tired.
I am tired of the nightmare.
You're lost!
You're lost!
No more anger!
No more anger!

I stop for a second to catch my breath. The energy I had in the beginning is depleting but the music keeps playing.

Clear thought!
How can I stop my mind from turning?
You're lost! The child you once were has turned into a something poisoned.
Toby, listen to the whole CD.

I sit down and give my feet a rest. I think about the gypsy and how she is just like the system. She laughs at me constantly. I can't find truth with her. I can't find it.

My favorite song comes on. I muster up some strength because this is the last round. I give it everything. I want to sweat out the poison in me. Get it all out. This is the last song.

I can feel the music and the leaves are dancing too.

I keep butting heads with them.
I keep butting heads with them.
Come on, is that all you have?
Is mercy a gift?
My anger builds up and I am sick of being angry, I don't want it.
It keeps building.
As it hits the climactic spot I see the crimes of man. There is no mercy.
I keep punching and punching and the music stops.
I'm standing there with hypocrisy flowing.
Quarterback, white asshole.

Tears start as I realize how thick my sickness is tonight. I'm on the ground with my hands holding me up and my feet are swollen from the steps I took on the solid dirt trail. Tears are coming. No more anger! I'm sobbing like a child. It feels so good to cry and feel something so strong. I am too thick.

What is wrong with me? I am sick.

Suddenly, I feel my father and how he was a good man and cared about people early in his life.

I am gone, father.

I am just here.

I see the gypsy laughing at me and I am sick of her.

She was so calming in the beginning.

I don't want her in my head anymore.

I punch my face as hard as I can. No more anger! I hit myself in the eye. I will set her free! (I hope the punches don't hurt her.) I have to get her out of my head.

I punch again as hard as I can.

And again.

And again.

And again.

The adrenaline is there. How am I going to explain this?

My face starts to hurt and I wonder if the gypsy hurt herself too.

She is gone now and I was left with a moment of clarity.

I was sick and I finally realized I needed help from someone.

The walk back was long and I felt hopeless.

I thought, maybe I could go to my Mom's house and show her my face and tell her to put me into an institution or something. Maybe I needed some kind of medication.

I went to my apartment, got in my car and drove to my Mom's house. She and my sister were still up. When I walked in they both looked at me in horror. There was some sort of strange satisfaction when I saw the looks on their faces. I looked at myself in the mirror and just above my temple my forehead looked huge like Frankenstein. My Mom got her keys and her purse.

We drive to the hospital and I think she is in denial about how bad I am. She doesn't know about the poison and how strong it is getting. We go through the steps, and some joker Doctor sees me. He asks me questions and I know how to answer them. I don't want to go to the mental institution. I can work it out. None of my.......

Muttle

Muttle

Muttle

Muttle

I did it. I fooled them all. I can go home now and take care of myself and help save the world.

# 20

## Pop Star

A new night--my brother calls me. I think it's because my Mom has told him how worried she is about me.

I keep seeing my counselor but I don't trust him. I know he can read my thoughts.

I am driving down to Colorado Springs to see my brother. As I make my way to my brother's house, I see a guy that looks like a famous musician driving in the car next to mine. He is driving the same kind of car that my brother drives? I walk into my brother's house; I see Cassias, his dog. I freaking love this dog. As I am sitting here I can feel the presence of a pop star. It is the same one I saw driving earlier in a twin car of my brother's. There's another pop star. And there's a third pop star. They are musicians that I admire. I can feel them the same way I can feel the gypsy. I can see a party in my brother's backyard with famous people all laughing at me and it pisses me off.

I don't want this. I don't want people wondering what I'll do next because I am crazy.

My brother puts on a movie. His girlfriend walks in and I say, "Hey." All three pop stars are still hiding in the backyard. I look at my brother and see Peter, Jesus' disciple. He acts like he knows a secret that I don't. Here I am trying to watch the movie with my brother and his girlfriend and the gypsy and all three pop stars are still in the backyard. Confusion--mass muttling my brain. It is time for me to go.

As I am driving I finally see a character that looks like one of my favorites, namely me. A roaring thunder comes out of my mouth and I say, "What is wrong with you, Toby."

Suddenly one of the pop stars starts talking to me, which is confusing because that means I am talking to myself. I am in the car alone. I have a double conversation with the pop star and it is real. I can't doubt it. There is fire in the air.

He says, "Nothing is wrong with you."

I say, "Screw you, you don't know."

I realize that the words coming from my mouth are the same words coming from his and we are both locked in this reality. Or is it fantasy?

I tell him, "Get out of my head."

I can't tell at this moment if it is him or me talking out loud, and I picture him in a room coked up and not knowing if it is he or me saying things. So I start to rant and I don't care what's said.

I ask him, "What do want from me?"

He asks me, "What do you want from me?"

I tell him, "Man, I don't want anything from you. I just want to be myself."

Did he say that or did I?

I keep ranting, "You people, you rock stars, you make people feel bad."

He asks me, "How do we make people feel bad? I play music because I love it."

Did I say that?

# muttle

I said that.

My mind hurts because I am speaking but my words don't seem to mean anything.

I yell at him, "I just know my dreams can't come true."

He says to me calmly, "You have to make it happen and if it doesn't then there is more to life than music."

I am still yelling, "You guys make me feel bad but I dig your music. Get out of my head. Are you talking or am I?"

He snidely says, "You're the one doing the talking. Think."

I scream, "Get out of my fucking head!"

I swerve all over the road and he's gone.

I keep driving and driving and I know the artists that are good have to love what they do and there is nothing wrong with a good show. But, when dreams die, it is hard to find the will to live and nothing hurts more than to give it everything and not be heard.

I wonder if this experience is real. It is real! I know it is real. I can feel the presence of people everywhere. This is energy that is outside of me. The machines have gotten into me.

I can feel the gypsy and she feels like she is mine. I feel like I can take care of her. The rest of the ride home I cut off the pop star and I get swept up in the gypsy. We are connected and whatever I go through, she goes through. I then think about Diana and how much more real she is to me. I get home and I am so tired I can barely hold onto the wheel. Is the connection there? I have to test it. It is late. I burn another cigarette hole in my foot. What will I become?

On this night I don't feel like walking. I just lay on the couch. The depression of where I am makes me so low that I can't take it anymore. I think about killing myself. I am so close to the end of my madness that I want it to be over. I decide it is time for me to do it and leave the world behind me. I have a picture in my head of hanging myself in my room. I can do it tomorrow. I will find a large hook and hammer it into the ceiling. I can then tie a rope around it and my madness will end. As I am laying on the couch I picture what it would look like. All of a sudden a strong man pushes his way into my thoughts. He takes the rope off the hook. He comes from nowhere. I didn't think him up he just invaded my vision. He says, "You don't need to do that son." There is wisdom in him that makes my heart blossom and I don't know who he is. What does he want from me? I am so tired.

The next day I realize that I can't kill myself. Not yet at least. There are too many things full of life and love that I see and I can't leave Jayde behind.

# 21

## Climbing

(Two months after my father died)

Everyone at work looks at me like I'm a lunatic and their words cut through me. Lisa came up to me and asked me if I was okay. She said that I had been standing in one spot for ten minutes wiping it with the rag and staring off into space. I told her, "Yes, of course I'm OK." Lisa and I are simpatico in so many ways but even she doesn't know what I'm turning into.

I know I'm hurting the people around me but I can't stop and I don't know how to stop. I feel good and I put my earphones on. I start walking and listen to a good band. They have such a chill groove. Their beats are simple but the base makes it nice. I walk through the intersection without looking and I don't care if a car hits me. There is blindness in my stretch across the street. I know the car will stop and if he doesn't, "Oh well." As I walk home I meander down to the usual park next to my apartment. I am going to just sit there and let my mind flow in two streams. There is a section by the park that has paved cement steps. There is one spot where I always sit. You can tell I have been there by the black circle of burnt out cigarette's and the ashes I leave behind. I sit down.

I always go back and forth between different styles of music. Rolling base lines have a sound that brings an Irish kind of poverty to mind. The songs are warm but the baseline pushes waves like the tide coming in. I think it is time to start walking again. I walk into our apartment and no one is there. I grab my backpack and put a blanket in it. I am going to the highest spot on Table Mountain today. As I walk out the door I am welcomed by the landlord. He's a cheery fellow. He talks to me but all the words are mixed up in my head and it feels like he said he is going to kill me one day. Is that what he said? Think clear, and get rid of the poison or bury my mind under my feet.

I move on and as I walk through the neighborhoods of Golden I see an old man shooting at me over and over with a rifle. Things will be different once I reach the trail head. By the time I get there it is night time and I know that the march is on. The walk to the base of the trail is mellow as usual and I think about the same walk I made with the bubbles of reincarnation floating around. The pictures of my landlord are gone because my head is down and I am concentrating on the steps. They are big steps and I can feel my legs getting tired.

I remember about a week ago how I was in the same spot going the other direction heading home. The rain started poring down and lightning was everywhere. I was stuck because I had no car. It isn't a long walk but it is when lightning is grazing your ear. The weather seemed to affect my mood. The little dry spots splotched on the streets were a perfect place to get hit by lightning. That would be a great way to die. As I walked, my old pastor came to mind. I call him Paul, because he was so strict. I think of the scripture where it talks about obeying the government and then I think of Hitler. Everyone in Germany who followed Hitler did the right thing according to the Bible. Jesus was the one who said, "Give unto Caesar what is Caesar's." We should only give the government what is necessary. I liked that. I could never completely pledge to any government, I am proud to be an American with all the gifts it brings but the two party system doesn't work, it just brings chaos and fickle minds with no compromise. Our so-called freedom is nothing more than a lie. We are bound by rules and regulations which lock us in a box.

I thought that on this day I'm going to make the journey again. I made it past the trailhead but I am going to go further up the hill and see what is lying there for me. I want to stand on the cliff of the pillars and look down at the small city below. I find peace on Table Mountain and I almost feel like me. The music is pulsing and right now it leads me to kind places. I had been taking big steps and I am where the steps had turned into a soft trail. It's a long way up Table Mountain and I think about what could be up there. I see a vision of dark maroon skies and I know that I have to walk it. I have to walk it because there are no dark maroon skies, only a black sky with calculated dots of white. I keep making the march. I don't feel chosen now. I think that is why I am pulling myself away from the reality of the world. I am walking away from everything. The night feels good and the darkness is welcoming me. I keep walking and I make my way to where the giant pillars of rock stretch around the whole mountain.

I think of a scientific expedition. Well, tonight isn't a scientific expedition but more of an observation. Not on science. Science is bound by rules and regulations. Religion is bound by rules and regulations. Forget it. It is time for me to keep going. As I make it to the top I decide to run the mild trail. If only the poison could come out. I am running so fast that my knee gives out but I am so out of control that there's a possibility that I could hurt myself. I can see by the reflection of the moon. I am pouncing from place to place through the rocky zigzag trail. I can see myself from the outside and I look like a warrior about to catch his prey. I am just a driven man pulling at strings of bushes and pouncing on ledges. I am going to observe the reality of a driven man. I faceplant and my mouth is filled with rocks. I spit them out and look up over a city of lights and I scream, "Where are your lights? Where are your lights? WHERE ARE YOUR LIGHTS?" As I stand I notice that my fingers are covered with blood (a minor wrinkle during this night of observation). Solid ground makes me sick. There are so many steps to take and I am not Adam or Eve tonight. There are no goddesses or gods, only something looking back at me.

I keep walking and wander to the spot where I drank fresh water and had a white lab for a companion.

The further I go the closer I get to a pit that looks man-made. It's at the peak of the mountain. It looks like it could be nature made. It reminds me of Italy and some of the giant pillars that man carved. I push myself further and the machines are gone. I am standing on top of the mountain with the pillars below me. I find a good rock to sit on so I can see everything. Someone made markings on the rocks next to me. I wonder if it is the gypsy. I don't understand them so I try to ignore them. I'm looking at Golden with a glimmer of hope at what I could be. I wonder what it will be like when there are no resources left and there are no crops to grow and the standing man-made pillars are left empty. I dream of a time when all the banks foreclose on all the houses and the people are in the streets. I see that day and I wonder if people will make the march. Not a sacred one like the one to Mecca but one to the White House. I see people sharing water. I see people picking each other up. I see old men on the backs of strong young people. I see a walk-for-change--a walk for a new way of life.

I take my blanket out because it is starting to get cold. Fall is coming and it will be nice to see some snow. I wonder if there is another man on another planet or star as twisted as I, wrapped in a blanket, starving himself, but digging.

My eyes are heavy and I wake up in a panic. I have to go home. I can't sleep on this drowning rock. I am going home. Anxiety hits me and I feel like I can't be in my own space anymore. I have got to get off this mountain. I start the long trek down and it's challenging getting from the rock I slept on to the trail. I can't see anything and I don't feel any peace. I pass some bushes and the light reflecting on them makes me jump. As I make my way around the mountain I look at the pillars of rock that stand to my left. I am almost to the trailhead and a light flickers from a house. It flashes many times. Could that be the gypsy? I stop and look at the house. I put my hand on my chest and turn my back on the light at the window. I turn my back on you, gypsy. I continue on through the bushes. The night is so dark. I look over to the left at the walls of rock and they make strange shapes. It isn't a hallucination. Shadows. I hate these shadows. I finally

get to the point where the trail starts down the mountain.
Muttle
Muttle
Muttle
Muttle

I am so close to home I can almost see it. The darkness has enveloped me and I have to get back home-home-home. I walk up the stairs and say Hi to Bob Dylan. I am tired and dirt follows me into the house. I lie down on the couch and have the whole place to myself. I am going to sit in front of the TV and fall asleep. I turn on PBS because it's always relaxing to watch something that isn't in my head. I sure as hell can't watch some sitcom where they are talking to me. I wish people would stop talking to me and I wish they couldn't hear my thoughts. They can't hear my thoughts. Toby, you're crazy. No one knows. But I know they do.

My eyes start to get heavy and the Ken Burns show comes on. They are talking about a man named Jack Johnson. I think to myself. This isn't the same Jack Johnson (the singer, song writer). No fucking way he has a PBS episode about him. My brain starts turning and I am glued to the TV. The man starts talking about boxing and the screen shows clips of black and white footage. It is older than the 50's black and white films. The frames are dirty. The story of Jack Johnson is told. It is a story of true adversity; an adversity that speaks loudly about the unjust, mean world I live in. Jack Johnson was the first African American to box for the championship, I think. I was having problems listening to the TV. The crowds in the clips were all white people and Jack Johnson's opponent was a large white man with a gruff look on his face. The fight lasted many rounds. Jack Johnson knew he could lay this guy out in a second but he played the crowd so they wouldn't 'string him up.' He beat the guy up and people were in an uproar. Riots broke out everywhere in the US and black people were being hung for mindless reasons. The film ended showing Jack Johnson with all new clothes and a cool hat. He was looking quite dapper and there was a big grin on his face. I fucking loved it. It sucks that there has to be sacrifices made in order for a man to distinguish himself, but the sacrifices were made and Jack Johnson distinguished himself. The same shit goes on today. It isn't fucking fair the way that people in poverty, black or white, are put down. There is a sign of redemption in the story of Jack Johnson. There is a sense of victory over the stigma of race.

It is about 4 A.M. I doze off. I wake up at 6 A.M. and I think about what the Jack Johnson movie symbolizes. I have to go to work at 2 P.M. so I guess I will go walking. While I walk, I decide that tonight after work will be a fun night, a night of self sacrifice.
Muttle.

Saving the world? Superman has that covered. I am just tired and I want a little personal satisfaction; something to make me smile again. Could I find my true smile without contempt? I go to work.
Muttle
Muttle

# 22
## A Beating

I'm at work.

Dan keeps talking to me and his words and stories are so fucking long and his lips are like daggers. I want to tell him to shut the fuck up.

Muttle

Muttle

Muttle

My shift is over and I am still feeling like the gimp cow in the herd that can't follow everyone else. The night has purpose and I know what I have to do. I have my bottle of drugs sitting by my bed in case I fail with my plan. My plan is suicide so fuck it-let's put God to the test again.

I am in my new car driving down the road. I know what I have to do. The intensity writhes and there is only one place I can image where four young black men could be waiting to give a "white boy" the beating of his life. I also know the right word to say. Colfax Avenue is sweaty and dirty as usual. I have taken the trip downtown many times. I am, of course, listening to a fearless band on my CD player. I picture in my head four young guys each with distinguishing features and I can see the anger on their brows and a passion in their eyes to kick my face in. Punch after punch -- blow after blow. I hope they fucking kill me because I am tired of this bullshit life and I will never find redemption. Going out like that would be perfect. They wouldn't get caught and I would just be a guy who died on a street. Nothing chosen about that, just raw anger.

Keep driving, keep driving. There is no justice, there is no justice. My Mother always said, "Things aren't fair -- there is no justice and truth lies dying in the street." My mind is relatively clear and I have a small spurt of adrenaline, which I know will get stronger. I drive down the streets and the building lights are blinding. There are people gathered around because of a concert. Fuck, where can I go? I could go to Five Points. I turn the wheel and point my car in the right direction. Five Points is being bought out by rich white

America but right now it is still half ghetto. Wait, which direction is it? I am so spaced out sometimes. Just go right. Just go right. Oh, okay, I know how to get there. I push through all the avenues and I am there. I know I am there because there is 'Herbs'. It is close to 'El Chapultepec'. I love those jazz musicians. I spent so many nights there. I spent those nights listening to a beat that is meant only for a man who drinks music. I park in the empty parking lot and I am all alone. I feel like shit but the little spurt of adrenalin is still with me.

I can't do it. Toby, you are fucking crazy. Why the fuck do you want to get the shit kicked out of you? You already punched yourself in the face. Oh, but the sweet redemption of taking a beating like that. This country is led by white fucks. People of different races are without a chance. It's messed up and I am part of that drowning system.

I think of Jack Johnson. Crystal cars are all around me.

Fuck, maybe in the midst of my beating I will have a grin on my face. I sit in the car. I can feel the gypsy telling me where to go. She surprises me with her energy.

I feel the gypsy. I then see her meeting me at this corner and going with her to listen to the jazz music. It is a good thought.

"Toby, you're so fucking scared. Get out of the car."

"Toby, what kind of man are you?"

"Toby, you're a fucking waste!"

"Toby, you freak! Get out of the car."

I am angry at myself and my stupidity. Maybe the four black men will kill me. That would be so perfect. It will end this circle of madness. My madness of four parts, two parts, one part, churning.

Muttle

What if they leave me paralyzed? Well, it would fit but that would not be good.

The voice of the gypsy spits out of my mouth, "Toby,

you are so afraid!"

This last insult from the gypsy brings the craziness on and I am ready. I am sick of hearing the machines' voices. I hear them, but I don't actually hear them. They are lost and crippling my mind.

I hope the men keep beating me even when I say to stop.

The door opens. I am focused. I have a goal. It is time. "Do you have the balls to do it?"

Say the word and there will be broken bones and deep pain. I walk the streets up and down. There is a stale alleyway that has the usual bars on the windows, and patches of dumpster puss. I have walked three blocks and I don't see a soul.

"Toby, Toby, you are such a freak. I bet the four black men are sitting around in their house having some drinks and smoking some bud just like you would do if you weren't a crazy asshole."

Keep going. Keep going. Keep going.

I see a bar at the corner. It looks like a total dive. I figure I can go in there and have a bunch of drinks and forget. I don't know about anything anymore but I know enough about some things. The door opens and the entire place is packed with Hispanics. What a lovely bit of irony. I sit down at the bar and the guy next to me looks confused. I am sure he is thinking, "What the hell is a suburban, white, clean shaven, asshole with a grin on his face doing walking into our bar? Who is this guy?"

I say, "Hey" to him to make sure he speaks English, and he does. Suddenly the Mr. Toby charm comes on and he and I get into a conversation about getting electrocuted. He has had a few more beers than I, so I try to catch up. I look over at a couple of guys playing pool and have a panic attack. I visualize them hitting me over the head. Maybe I will get the crap kicked out of me tonight after all. The alcohol starts kicking in and the booze starts to mellow me out. My new friend decides to go over to the bar and talk with his buddy. I think about my friends and how everyone is so busy. It feels like I have lost my friends. Maybe they are just giving me space with my father's death. Space is one thing that I need. I sit there, finish my drink and then drive home.

I turn the radio off because it seems like the more music I listen to the crazier I get. I can't help it though. I shouldn't be driving, but I do. I start to get sleepy and I know that I will probably sleep tonight and tomorrow. Sleep is a good thing. I am hungry. I will just have a cigarette. I pull in the driveway and go into my apartment. I put the bottle of meds by my bed. Maybe tonight I will have the courage to end. My body is so tired. My head hits the pillow. No dreams.

# 23
## Ghosts

I wake up the next day and go to work. I feel like I am carrying the weight of the world on my shoulders. I feel like I have to just keep digging. Am I looking for my truth or the world's truth? I don't know how I can find anything with the muttle in my brain. I get off work and the whole day is in front of me. I am tired and this desire to hold myself up is leaving me with the feeling of being alone. I am trying to find myself and be whole again in this mess. I don't know who I am anymore because of the scrambled brain and the desire to be a wrecking ball and just destroy everything. I decide I want to let go of my music again and watch my dreams die in the wind. I take my CD's and head to Red Rocks. I don't want to give my music to God I just want to destroy it. I park in a space at Red Rocks that is close to the trail and close to the amphitheater. I have a backpack full of all my CD's. I find a trail below the theatre and start walking on it. There is a cave that is hidden from the people on the trail. I pull out my CD's and throw them as hard as I can against the wall of the cave. I will never make it in music and I want my dream to die. I want to throw away something beautiful. I keep throwing CD's and I break them into pieces. It looks like there is glass everywhere. I keep throwing them until they are gone and then pick up the broken shards of them and fill my backpack with them.

I carry my backpack to the stage. It is a long walk from the trail to the amphitheater's stage. As I am walking on the stage I open up my bag and broken shards spread everywhere. I hear someone yelling at me but I just keep walking. I don't want a confrontation I just want to leave my mark. I know I will never play Red Rocks so I leave what's left of my music on the stage. As I get into my car I feel good about letting my music go. The night passes and as the day roles into night the guilt hits me hard. I don't feel bad for breaking the CD's but I do feel bad for leaving them there for someone else to pick up. It's late and I decide that I want to go back and try to make things right. I wonder if the darkness will be there like before. I wonder if I will have the courage to face my fears. Before, when I went to Red Rocks, I went to give my music to God. But now I just want to destroy everything. I leave my apartment and have my harmonica with me. The drive to Red Rocks is glossy and the night air is cool. It is going to be Fall soon and I have to keep close to the summer like a magnet. I have been such a machine in my walking this summer. I find peace in my walks and yet there is still the muttle.

I park my car and I decide not to go in just quite yet. I find another trail that leads east of the amphitheater. There is a perfect spot to just sit and relax and look at Denver. I decide to try some meditation to relax my brain. In all this mess I have tried meditation and sometimes it works.

As I sit there alone in the darkness I see pictures while my eyes are closed. There are yellow lines moving around and strange pictures filling my mind. There isn't a solid picture. The lines keep moving fast.

I was meditating a couple days ago and I saw the strangest thing. I was sitting in the middle of the park with my eyes closed in the dark and all of the sudden the color purple was everywhere. My eyes were closed but the purple was solid. It changed to red and then the darkness came back. I was surprised at the vivid color and wondered if it meant something.

On this night the lines are there but I can't find peace in my mind. I am looking for a place where the center of me is constant and I can feel relief. I sit there for a long time being alone and feeling alone. I see my friends every once in a while but for some reason they just frustrate me because I can't be honest with them. I am a good actor and I do a fine job of being normal around them.

It is time to go to the stage. I have an extra kick in my step and feel like there is something waiting for me. I get inside the amphitheater and it is huge. There isn't anyone around that I can see from the stage. I go to the stage with my backpack and try to find the broken pieces. They aren't there. Someone must have picked them up. I decide to take my harmonica out and play on the stage. I realize that there is no difference between the musicians that play and the crowd that listens. There is talent on the stage but there is talent in the audience. So I decide to play my harmonica from the stage to the last seat of the theatre. It is a long walk going upstream. I walk from left to right on the first row and then walk from right to left on the second row. My harmonica is playing the whole time. It is going to be a long walk but I have to make it. I keep walking and I am on row 10 when I see something bizarre.

Above me about thirty rows there is a girl in a white dress that is running back and forth from one side to the other. I think about the gypsy and wonder if it is her. She is running so fast. Then there are several girls with white dresses that are running across. This is too bizarre and I can't help but wonder if it is someone making the same point as me, saying that there is no difference between the performer and the crowds. The girl with her long dress is running fast and I keep playing my harmonica. When we are about five steps away from each other I ask her if she is having fun. She stops and looks at me with an intense look like what we are doing is not a joke. I don't recognize her. I take one more step up and the girl I see now looks like the gypsy. I get a close look at her. She has the same body type and I can feel her. There are several girls but maybe there is just one. Maybe these white dressed girls are ghosts. Maybe they are angels.

So we get to the point where she is at the row right next to me. I am excited that I can finally match up a face with this strange situation. As I am walking with my harmonica blaring loud, a man with his shirt off passes me. I guess the ghost doesn't want me to see her face. So I keep going. I have to finish what I started. The ghosts are gone and it is just me. I wonder many things about this night. As I finish my last row I start to take the march back down to my car. As I am walking out of Red Rocks I see a car parked with its lights on and wonder who it could be. A ghost car? The gypsy's car? If only I could just find answers and not more questions. Where do I fit in this puzzle? I get in my car and go home. I am tired from the day and I haven't slept much or eaten anything for a while. I will just go home and find some rest. Maybe tomorrow my questions will be answered and maybe not. Maybe God is trying to speak to me in these signs and omens.

The next few days pass. Caleb and Andrea invite me to their church. It is on the east side of Denver and I meet them at their house. It is a special day at the Church. The services are outside at a park that I have never been to. There is a huge gazebo that has tons of picnic tables set up for lunch. The service itself is outside the gazebo where they have lined up chairs for all the people. The message the pastor gives is good but my mind is wandering. It is hard to focus on exactly what he is saying. There is a stream next to the gazebo. After the service we all line up at the picnic tables and eat burgers. I had been to the church before and know a few people. After we eat the band plays music next to the picnic tables. The roof is high and the space is big enough for everyone to sit or stand. As the band starts playing the strangest thing happens: I picture myself floating on a cloud in the air below the roof. I can't see the cloud. All I see is me floating in a Zen state. I am sitting like a monk meditating and all the music that is playing is being played for me, like everyone is worshiping me. It is hard to look at and I sit there and watch it for thirty seconds. I feel so elated and eventually I can't let myself feel worshiped, so I walk away. My blasphemy is overwhelming and I feel sick. I can't control my thoughts. It isn't my fault. I sit at the stream and try to forget feeling regret. I then realize that I can never go to church again unless it is absolutely necessary.

I wish I had the clarity of mind to keep my focus strong but I don't. My mind is like a bulldozer going wherever it wants with remorse following it. I have to let it go somehow but don't know how.

# 24
## Miner

The day after church I get out of work in the mid afternoon and wonder what the day will bring.

I walk over the bridge in my park and I see the same statue that I have looked at many times before. The Native American woman is there and she has seen me at my lowest and highest. The artistic quality of her is amazing. If you get close to her she almost speaks to you.

I feel like a train huffing along because of all the cigarettes I am smoking. It feels like free will and destiny have collided in me. I am trying to feel free while I am guided. I walk up Clear Creek and find a rock to sit on by the stream. The gypsy is playing tricks in my head and planting things that shouldn't be there. I am pissed because the whole person I used to be has become two halves chasing after each other. I am listening to some music and I see an old man across the stream moving rocks. His face draws me to him and I ask him how he is doing. (There is another man I run into on my walks and he is always carrying his fishing pole.

I tried to talk with him but he just glared at me.)

The man who is moving stones says, "Hi" and asks me if I want to help him. I am so starved for wisdom that I walk over the bridge upstream that separates us and down a random trail to meet him. I almost fall because it is so steep. We are surrounded by huge rocks and I ask him what he is doing. He says, "Panning for gold." I get a little closer to him and he has some gear that looks interesting. My mind is still turning and thoughts are coming from a place that is not me. He tells me to move some rocks. So I hunch down in my sandals and move one. His equipment includes an interesting rectangular frame with filters in the middle. He takes the dirt from under the rocks and the dirt goes through the frame. We spend a couple hours working and talking. He is an interesting guy and he asks me why I look so upset. I didn't realize that I looked upset so I tell him that I don't know. He then tells me: "Look at the colors. They are waiting for you."

We talk about society and all the same old stuff. He tells me that he used to work for NASA. Well, that is as believable to me as UFOs. But, hey, maybe he did. Maybe he didn't. He has to deal with his own conscience and his own lies. He tells me that I am in the 5th percentile. He says that everyone else is in the 95th percentile, but that I am not. He tells me that I am different. I say, okay, and the numbers start rolling around in my head. I can't comprehend 5. We keep talking and he tells me his last name, which is Italian. He says it means messenger, which sounds intriguing. Maybe he is here to tell me something. Maybe the wisdom I am looking for he can give. So we keep working and the conversation continues.

He looks at me sharply and says Bill Gates has got it right. He doesn't say anything after that which to me means Bill Gates has got it right because he is rich or because he found a way to live life with no cares. Maybe Bill Gates worries more than anyone. We keep talking and working.

# muttle

The miner looks like a mix between Santa Claus and Willie Nelson. He is wearing overalls and wet boots. His shirt is red plaid and he has an immense amount of energy and strength for a man in his seventies. We start packing all of his things and we make our way to his car. He asks me if I want to smoke some pot. I haven't smoked in a while but I wonder if it will help me think clearer. I wonder if it will solve whatever poison is in me. When we are stoned, words start coming out of our mouths. It is almost like we have known each other before. He starts talking like he is God, and I mean the Christian God. Then he switches it around like the nature of God is something new or Buddhist. I am talking to him the whole time and I can't figure out if he is saying things or if I am just imagining it. The conversation lasts for a while and before I know it I realize that I am having a drug induced hallucination, which is welcome because it makes me not see black and white so much.

I tell the miner that he looks like Santa. He starts laughing and so do I. I begin to confide in him about the stuff going on in my head. He asks me if I had ever seen the movie 'Groundhog Day' and I tell him, "Yes, it is one of my favorite movies." He then tells me, "You just have to keep going until it fits and it is right. You will see the colors.: In my mind I wonder if reckless thoughts will ever cease to be reckless. I get out of the car and he goes his way and I go my way. He seems like a good guy. He seems like an avenue to wisdom.

The machines.

I spend about a week hanging out with the Messenger.

He keeps talking about all the little pieces of gold; the tiny piles of gold just waiting to be found. It symbolizes heaven in my mind. Each piece of gold is an individual. I am not sure what it symbolizes to him. He also talks about how you have to pick up a rock sometimes and move it to find the gold. In my head I am thinking of the analogy of moving mountains with your faith compared to moving rocks and finding gold. I wonder and think about the times in my life I have had faith. Those times were like drops from heaven laughing as they hit the ground. He starts telling me that he can move at the speed of light and that an Asian monk taught him how to do it. It sounds interesting. I constantly look at him to see if he is moving around at the speed of light. Now, I don't actually believe that the guy can do it but maybe he is connected like the gypsy. There is a twinkle in his eye when he says it and I want to believe him.

Our ritual is to work the stream and clean up. As we go to the car to smoke our ritual pot, he starts talking about sex with a red head and how it is so great. He then looks at me as if it is something I will do and smiles. He then says that I will have to choose between two girls but they have to come to me. This rings true because I am drawn to the gypsy, but I talk with Diana every day at work.

I decide that this will be the last day I spend with the Messenger.

I go back to my apartment and I play a little music.

I don't know why I don't drink alcohol anymore.

The window is open and I know I didn't open it.

Muttle
Muttle
Muttle

I wonder if it moved by some force that I have let in. It seems letting in the gypsy and letting in the miner have caused more stress than two wheels turning on a road of sand paper. I am all cranked up about it and I don't know how to explain it. The whole night I sit in my room waiting for something else to happen. I am closed off from everything.

Frustration builds to anger and I want to take hold of reality. I want it to be like a piece of rock in my hand that I can hold on to. I again leave my room, my apartment. I start walking and I want to tell the miner and the gypsy to screw off. I don't need this and I choose reality not to be chosen.

I walk to a bar in Golden. I am not wearing my hoodie and it is cold. I sit in the bar and stare at a wall. I don't know how to shake all this off, so I ask for another drink. As I am staring at the wall, I see pictures of Native Americans. If I had only one small drop of Native American blood, would it be enough to fight off the poison that seems to have taken hold of me?

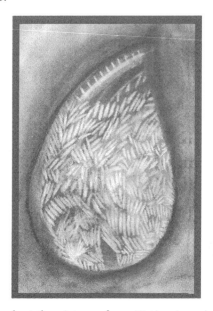

I look at the picture of one Native American and we stare at each other. I wonder what he sees looking at me; a white hypocrite who can't appreciate anything? I see him as a warrior, a man who chooses his destiny and follows his tradition.

I leave the bar and I wish so hard for that one little drop of Indian blood. I walk and start marching at a fast pace. I don't want it anymore. I see a plant that has knobs on the end and I hit it. The same moment I hit it, a fish jumps out of the water.

What was that?

Anger starts building because I am so tired and I am a man who has to find some control. In the dark I find the trail that leads to the spot where the minor and I work. I pick up as many rocks as I can and throw them down as hard as I can.

"What do you want from me, old man?"
"What do you want from me, old man?"
"What do you want from me?"

I feel strength in my throbbing vocal chords. Throwing down the rocks is burning the poison out. I decide to head back to the trail.

I am standing next to the Native American Statue. It has been mocked so many times by so many people. I have a desire to be connected to this beautiful princess. I push my way up on the pedestal that holds her and I say to her. "Is this what you want me to do? Do you want me to be crazy? Well, then, FINE!" I lean in and the statue looks alive. As I face the statue I want to be angry but instead I kiss her softly on the lips. When I start to pull away there is something on the other side that kisses me back. Maybe the earth is covered with a maze of machines and electricity that we don't know about. I ponder. After kissing her and jumping down from the pedestal she sits on, I find myself laughing at what would lead me to do this, but the heart of the earth gave me a spark. I want to kiss her again. I felt peace for a moment. I saw a light. I turn and walk over the bridge.

I can't stay in this house tonight. I start making the trek up to Table Mountain. My mind is relatively clear now and it is so strange that some things set me off and some things chill me out. I walk around the base and up the trail. I go to the top and my eyes are on the stars the entire way up. I wonder if we are here to fulfill a purpose. I wonder if this planet is chosen. Maybe it just keeps going but our paths come to an end. Maybe the anti-christ is just someone who God has turned His back on but maybe he (the anti-christ) could show us the colors. If he turned his back on God how can he have power? Maybe I am here to show people the colors. All men and women die. I have seen signs, omens, and divinations. I have crossed borders and I stand here on this magnificent mountain and ponder eternity. I think of the little things that keep it all going. I want to touch every little thing that I see. It is chilly and the night stars are bright because the moon is nowhere to be found. I am alone as usual. I look down at my moles and I look up at the sky and they feel like two walls saying hello. Maybe in my moles I will find my way out of this mess.

I stay there for a time. My home has become a place that other men won't lay their heads, rocks and dirt. This home of mine is getting colder and colder. I could walk to the pillars or the rock that I drank water from. I think I will stand closer to the edge. I wonder what it is like to fly, to let go and flap your wings. I am not insane enough to take the leap. If there is enough faith to move mountains maybe my faith could be so strong that I could fly, but the Bible says to not test God. It is that whole gravity thing that gets in the way. I love my insanity because I would never have a night like this without it and I hate my insanity because I am not whole. I see strange markings on some rocks again. I wonder if the gypsy left them for me. I look at them and I see nothing.

# 25
## Throwing a Stone

**A**nother morning comes. My brother is visiting today. He doesn't know how sick I am right now and I can't tell him. My big brother would just say, "Put it in a box." I wish it was that simple.

We walk around Golden and I show him the town. *He has a look in his eye that is disturbing. It isn't a look like the sad coffee customers. I see a spark that I haven't seen before and in my mania I know he has seen the gypsy. I look into his face and look into his eyes and there is some magic there. My brother has a gruff face but he looks so beautiful. His green eyes are magnified and radiant. The gypsy got to him? Could this be not real?*

After walking around town we go to a restaurant. He orders fish and I have the same thing. I love fish and the fact that I live in Colorado sucks because we can't get fresh fish. We talk about the usual stuff. We always talk about books and random things. Our meal arrives and I feel like he and I caught the fish and are sitting down to enjoy a hard day's work. I feel like a fisherman and there is nothing in this world that I would rather feel like right now. He tells me about a recent case of his. I always love to hear about the people he is defending. There are different types of criminals and he knows all of them. After he has paid for our fish, we stand outside talking and I tell him that I believe in fate and there has to be a reason for the things that happen to us. He laughs, not in a condescending way but more like, I am going to challenge my little brother. With simplicity he says, "Maybe there is nothing. Maybe there is only now."

He drives me home. I love this guy so much and I want him to be happy. He goes with the flow and I pray that he never has to face a tidal wave. Before he leaves he says something about a girl. *I can't quite understand it because of the muttle. He leaves and I find myself trapped in the apartment. I can't bear it and I go outside. The rest of the day I walk around my park burning people down and bringing them back with my smokes. I can't control it. I don't know why it feels so real, but it does. I keep walking and I think about the gypsy and how I have become a stalker. I have not tried to make real contact with her so I am not a stalker. No, I am not a stalker. I can feel the energy. It is too strong to just "put in a box."*

*My body feels good. I go back to the apartment and see my roommate, Kelly. He is getting his cycling gear on. It is strange how he and I always loved the Jack Kerouac thing. Traveling and backpacking through Europe was like living a bum's life.*

*I am so marred by what's going on in my brain. I wish for the confidence and balance I used to have. Sure, I have been lazy in my life but I always had confidence. It is like I am myself but there is a raging storm in my head.*

*Kelly and I listen to music and chill. It is good when he is around because I am forced to act normal.*

*The day leads into the night and I have this sick feeling in my gut. It feels like the gypsy is with my brother and it is my fault. It feels like I am to blame for this betrayal. It is late and normal people are in bed, but I still feel her with my brother. His eyes were so bright. I get in my car and drive as fast as I can to Colorado Springs where* my brother lives. It is an hour drive. When I look in the rearview mirror, I see a skeleton. It is me. I am starving myself. I don't mean to do it. I am just not hungry. Smoking has taken the place of eating.

I am on I-25 and my body starts to shut down. I can barely hold my hand on the wheel but I know I have to save my brother from the gypsy. I feel like I am going to explode like a balloon. My hand starts shaking and before I know it my whole body is shaking. I see my death and I will end when I make it to my brother's house. I can feel it with my limbs. I am dying. I have to pee. I am listing to Bob Marley. I finally get to a rest stop and I pee. Strange! All the anxiety left when I pissed.

I still see me dead in the front of my brother's house. I start driving again. I feel sick because I trust my brother but who could resist a 'siren.' I drive faster and I get mad at my brother. I want to say something to him. I want to say, "Wake up." Is there any way that he will hear me? When I make it to my brother's house I realize that death has not come for me. There is a huge cement block just lying in the front yard. I take the block and throw it through the front window. I turn to run to my car and then it dawns on me: What if I hurt Cassius? I love that dog. My brother loves that dog! I go back and see my brother inside. I yell at him and he realizes that it is me. He swings open the door and tells me to come inside. We have this strange bubble hanging over our head. He is confused. He knows I am crazy but when I threw the block, I crossed a line. He offers me food and we play chess. The sun is starting to come up and he wants me to stay. I can't find the 'siren' in his house but it sure feels like she is here. I tell him I'm sorry for what I did and I ask him if I can pay for the window. He, of course, says no. I want to stay but I know it's time to go. He asks me again if I want to stay. I tell him I will be okay. I leave with my eyes watery because I love him so much. The drive back is sweet melancholy. Light blue sky gazes over the foothills as the sun comes up. I am falling apart and I'm not sure how much longer I can take it. And what will I do when I can't take it anymore? I could kill myself!

Not a bad idea.

# 26

## Perversion

So, I threw a brick through my brother's window (it was more like a cinder block). What was wrong with me? *Stop, wait Toby. I have an imaginary girlfriend. The energy is always talking to me. The circles I make don't have an exit. They are tight and as confining as a box. They still go round.*

I have to go to a party for the foster kids. It's been a few days since I threw the brick through my brother's window. I think my brother told my mom because she is worried about me. The party is huge and we spend the first couple hours blowing up balloons. The party is at a ranch and there is a hay ride, horses, and all kinds of booths for the kids.

I wander around and look all the booths over but mostly I am looking at the foster children. I have the poison in me but I am trying to help the kids and just relax. At the hay ride there is a little girl that seems sad. She looks like she has taken on a burden too big for a child. I guess the hurt these foster children know is beyond my hurt. I deal with what I deal with, but these kids feel hopeless because they have been rejected by the people in their lives that mean the most to them. I want to reach out to the little girl but I can't. My own distortion won't let me say any more than hello and what's your name. I hope that whoever takes care of her gives her what she needs. As a parent or an uncle it is easy to let things slip with kids and not give them what they need.

I keep moving around the crowd and I find myself talking with the director of the organization. He's a nice man. I want a job where I am not swilling coffee. I wish he would hire me to market his product which seems to be an escape for rejected children.

The party is a success. My mom made sure that my niece, Jayde, made it to the party and she absolutely loved riding on the horses.

It was quite a shindig and there were so many things for a kid to do. I was put in charge of the sumo ring. It was fun just watching the kids get into the suits. My mom wanted to introduce me to another foster child but my heart was still with Gabriel. For some reason that little kid touched me and I still thought about him. I had seen him earlier in the day.

My mom insisted on me meeting this new child. He was disfigured and I felt the poison pulsing in my heart. *I can see the perversion of the world in this poor little kid. I see it and I am spinning like a drunken man in a circus.*

*There is a huge horse standing there and I look him in the eye. He jumps and starts going crazy. Did I do that?*

*I see Jayde on a horse and I keep my eyes on the ground because I don't want the horse to see my eyes. My eyes are void of something. I make a quick decision to leave.*

When I got home it was the middle of the day and I went for a walk. I walked up the stream to where the trail gets dark. I sat under the bridge where the homeless people stay. *I can see something in the sky. Now, I'm a Superman kind of guy and I always correlate Superman with Christ. As I stand there*

I see Superman flying but it is the heart of the Lord. I watch in awe because it is so real. The Being starts spinning around the sun. I am in awe of this being in the air but I am ready to not have bad chemicals that make him real. Maybe I am him. I start walking back and I get to my apartment. I still have the perversion with me-- perversion that has always been. I want it out of my system.

It is time for this to be gone. I go to the grocery store and buy cigarettes and then I buy a couple bottles of commercial cranberry juice. I take them all to my little park. I sit on the bench and know what I have to do. My mind has been so perverted in so many different ways and now I have found the cure. I hit play on the Mp3 player and I listen to good songs, good melodies. I start smoking. Now, this is not casual smoking. This is smoking. I smoke it down to the butt and then keep on going. I smoke as much of the butt as I can and it makes me gag. I keep smoking them like this and I feel like I am overcoming the perversion. I feel like I am changing myself. Butt after butt after butt after butt. I am smoking till my lungs fill with fire. The whole pack is gone and it is time for me to take the next step ridding myself of the perversion. Out of the gypsy's window I hear a girl's voice say, RUN. Evidence of the gypsy? Finally, I am not delusional. I start running and my sandals fall off. I let them go and am running with my bare feet. When I get to where the trees are thick I know that what I do will rid myself of the perversion. Now I'm walking and listening to music. I can feel waves flowing up and down. I am sailing on the wind and this mild hallucination tells me that I am going to the right place. The waves go up and down and I am one with the earth but my mind sits in a boat which is out at sea. I go to the miner's spot. His perversion was the start of the bad thought-- or was it the book, 'The Prophet?' I make my way down the steep trail where once I had fallen. I get to the spot where the trees part to make a clear path and bend under them to find the spot. As I sit in the spot I know it's time. It is time to get it out. The perversion is in my body and soul and this will do it. I start drinking the commercial cranberry drinks. I slam them down as fast as I can. I still have the taste of bad cigarette burning in my mouth. I am finally finished with the last one and I bend over and put my finger down my throat. Get the *perversion out. My finger is in my throat. Eventually, a red stream flows out of my mouth and when I look at it on the ground it looks like beautiful berries.*

*I grab a bottle and say, "No more lies, miner." I will bury your head today. My heart hurts and I am not myself. I break the bottle on the rocks and leave glass everywhere, which I hate because I am not a fan of littering. I take a piece of the glass and start cutting a line over my heart. I thought it would be easy but the glass pieces are dull.*

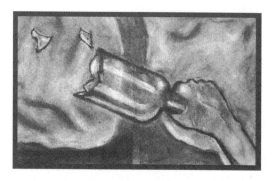

*I start cutting anyway. It takes a great deal of pressure to do it but I make my cut. Blood! That is what I want.*

*I start walking back without my shirt on knowing the perversion is not gone and wondering if I am the perversion. I walk by the gypsy's window and I am proud of the mark I make. I go home and I take a shower. I go for another walk. I go home. My friend Dustin shows up. He and I talk and I tell him how sick I am. Dustin is a good listener and it is good to see him.*

# 27
## The Drive

I got a job as a car salesman while I worked at the coffee shop. I had the energy to do it and I was going to do it. The reason I got the job was because I went with Mom to buy a car for her and the head loan officer remembered me from the coffee shop. He was impressed with me and the way I handled myself with customers and offered me a position on the spot.

The car dealership was a big one. The training process was nothing more than a group of men in suits gathered around trying to absorb information so that they could be super salesmen. The first day I walked in I knew it would be bad. The thing that had its grip on me was making it impossible to retain information. Everyone in the room was talking and bragging and I had a strange feeling that I had been there a thousand times before. The man sitting next to me talked through me. He was yelling and I couldn't understand why. The cloud in this place was growing and my vision was tired and muttled. I sat through the sessions and tried to make sense of it all. I was trying to be normal. Isn't that what everyone wants who has muttle seeping off them? It didn't work.

I laughed at the most inappropriate times.

We had to take the cars for a drive so that we would know what we were selling. I was stuck with the yelling man. *He tells me I have to choose between Diana and the Gypsy. He didn't actually say their names but insinuated both of them. He says one of them will die. I have no idea what he is talking about. I don't like what he is saying though and he is yelling everything he says. How can I get away from him? We drive the cars around like madmen to test them out and then find ourselves back at the dealership. There is a strange feeling in the room and the instructor starts asking me questions. My mind is in a new place. A place I have never been before. It feels like my head is cracked and my brain is spilling on the table. I am trying to hold the pieces together with my hands. I can't focus on his question. I sit there like an idiot and I'm sure he thinks I am. The thoughts I am thinking are reflections. It is like standing in front of one of those twisted mirrors at a carnival.*

On the first day of our training he had handed us a manual to help us learn the business. *I look at it and think it is The Revelation. Truth spills out of it. Not in headings but mostly in the text. I can't stop reading it. It is my new bible. I keep reading it and I take it home. The next few nights I study it and study it, looking for truth. I can't remember what it says from one line to the next but I can't put it down. I also feel like I am on death's door and it resonates in my bones. When the weekend comes, I put the book down and I have no idea what I have read.*

*The poison is still strong.*

*I hate this place. It reflects the hell of a madman.*

Selling cars is a good job for some but I couldn't do it. I told the trainer that I couldn't do it and he told me that he had this great idea for me. He said that I could work with an escort service company. I told him I wasn't interested.

*I go to the bank and ask for a new debit card. Today is the day that something amazing is going to happen. My birthday date* sticks out in my head; three sevens. I feel like I am lucky and have been chosen for something. I know the card is the answer. It has three sevens on it too. It has to be a sign. I put the card in my pocket and walk down to the stream to figure it out. It occurs to me that I should go to Las Vegas with my card. I can burn the whole place down and take every cent. I will give it to the poor countries of the world. I get in my car (I still have on my suit from my last training session) and it is time to drive. I haven't eaten or slept for a while so I figure I will have to stop on the side of the road to sleep. I start driving. Music is the key to this trip. It always gets me through. It is already late so I'm driving at night. I am buzzed and the drive is easy at first. It isn't like a road trip though; I feel a dread and wonder if I am going to die. At this point I want to drive myself into the ground. I want to see how far I can go. I push on and on and on and on. The music helps.

I hear sirens. The sun should be coming up soon but it is pitch black. There are sirens, the police kind. I pull over and a cop walks up to my car. He asks me what I am doing out so late at night and looks at my driver's license. He is surprised that I have driven all the way from Colorado. I tell him that my girlfriend and I just broke up and I have to drive. He tells me to pull over and get some sleep but after he goes back to his car I pull out and I keep driving. I eventually decide that pulling over is not a bad idea. I jump in the back and try to stretch out. I am saving gas so I don't want to leave the heater on. I wrap myself up in my business suit but it is no match for the cold. Fall is peeking its head on the dry hot land and I lay there while the poison starts pulling me down. There is no way I can sleep, so screw it, I keep going. I haven't slept for at least twenty-four hours but I haven't choked. I have smoked an endless amount of cigarettes.

I am behind the wheel and there is sort of glazed hypnotic state that I get into on this stretch of highway. The sun starts to come up and it feels like jars of honey. I keep going. Lack of sleep pushes me on. As I drive through the mountains I sit in awe of them. I think of all the things I will do with the money I will get from tearing down the casino walls. I think of all the countries that will be fed. I think of all the people renting that will own houses. I think of all the homeless that will find places for food and a bed. I am driven on this trip. I am a man that wishes to do the will of a Higher Power-- a fighter. I am so excited to tear Vegas down. I bartended at a casino in Blackhawk during college summers and I saw the zombies spending all their paychecks. It's time for me to help them get it all back. I keep going and I am ready.

It is daytime and the town is bright. I pull into the parking lot of the Excalibur and walk in. I am standing in front of the ATM machines and I put my card in one. My special numbers will take it down. I wait for the cash to start pouring out of the machine. I picture all machines in the world spitting money out. The machine has no magic and it reflects the real world. My head drops and I know my delusions are delusions.

I know I am a fool. I know the gypsy is nothing but bad energy,

I know I am sick.

# 28
## The Drive Home

*T*he walk out of the Excalibur to my car is a long walk. The lights, all these lights are supposed to be beautiful but they are bright and ugly. The people are not happy here. Look at them, they aren't having fun. They all look so worried and stressed. There is no laughter. There is no love for life. There is no hope. I was so positive that I could tear up the whole system. There is so much good that would have come from me destroying Vegas. All these faces would have been so happy and joy would have been in the air. There is only desolation and despair because of my failure.

I am so tired I can't believe it. My brain hurts and my body is weak. I get into my car and there is so much traffic. The machines outside of me talk to me and laugh at me. What a fool I am to think it could be that easy. I am frustrated with this town. As I finally get out of Vegas a panic hits me and I have a feeling that something has happened to my mom, sister, and niece. I know something has happened. What am I going to do? I have to get there as fast as I can. No, maybe I will just give them a call from my cell phone.

I pull the cell phone out of my pocket and make the call. My *mom answers and I ask her if everything is okay. She says, "Yes, and where in the world are you?" She has a worry in her voice that makes me feel guilty. I just sort of laugh and tell her that I'm on my way to my apartment. She has no idea that I am in Las Vegas, Nevada.*

*I start driving; it's time to go home. I'm on the right highway, I think. After about an hour of driving I realize that I have at least sixteen hours left to drive. What a dread -- especially when you haven't slept for two days. I push on and get to a small town. I don't remember this town. I have never been here. I stop to look at my map. I went the wrong way. No way. This sucks and I am so turned around.*

*I realize that the cops are after me. Shit, they know about my card that I put in the ATM machine and they are coming to get me. They can read my mind. Maybe the ATM worked. I know it. It's happening! If they can read my mind, won't they know that when I put my ATM card in, my intent was to steal from the rich? I don't know. I don't know anything. I feel like they are after me and I have to get out of here. I walk into a bar and peek around the corner to make sure there are no police officers. There is a short heavy guy at the bar and I ask him how to get to Denver. He tells me slowly like I am stupid. It makes me happy to have this moron treat me like a moron. I walk out of the bar. I get in my car and start driving. My map is a different language. It feels like it keeps switching around and my frustration turns into a realization that I will never get out of here. Finally I find the highway and there is a big sign that tells me where to go. I have many miles ahead of me.*

*I drive.*

Muttle

Muttle

Muttle

*Night is here and I am still hours away from Denver. This drive has been like a triathlon. I feel horrible and I haven't had food since the gas station in Vegas where I had a small piece of beef jerky. I did have some water with me but I feel like hell. What is wrong with me? Why don't I eat? I look like a beanpole from these last months of self destruction. I'm not doing it on purpose. I'm just not hungry.*

I suppose the cigarettes have something to do with it. I have smoked my way through this trip and they are getting me through it.

I finally make it into Colorado and now I have to drive through the Rocky Mountains. I know I can make it home. I just have to keep going. No sleeping. I can't sleep in this heap. My car is a hypocritical blimp. I just have to keep going. I see a star on the horizon and it helps me stay on track. It is straight in front of me and I have to drive through it to end this trip.

I keep driving and I turn the radio off because the sounds feel like crinkling cuts. I am so tired. It is the peak of my destruction. If only I were in a place called home. If only I could see my friends: Kelly, Lisa, Zane. If only I could see my family. My brother with his lawyer smarts, my sister with her helpful heart, my mom who I can always talk to and my Jayde who is the only reason I haven't put a bullet in my head. I am cold and not the kind of cold measured in degrees but more the kind of cold that sits in your stomach and reminds you, you're alone. I still see the star and I jerk up. I think of all the sailors out at sea. They know the kind of cold I speak of but have guiding lights that take them home. My thoughts are steady now and I have to push on. It is a straight path to Denver if I could only reach the star. The stars of the night seem brighter than usual and I try to keep going. My eyelids are falling and I think that I can't make it. I am going to be sick. I think I might have accomplished what I was so afraid to try -- the destruction of me. Death is knocking on my door and I think I am ready. Maybe that ATM card will come through and my brother and mom can make a mark in the world with a paper green horror that shows us the opportunity cost and the opportunity lost or gained. I am going to pull over because I am not that sailor who is guided home. I am the sailor left behind.

I pull off the highway at a restaurant. It is dark and the mountains take up the sky. They are dark, much darker than the sky. On the way to Vegas, the moon was reflecting on the mountains, but in this place I am buried. I looked up at a huge red sign (advertising what?) and it vibrates with a reality that I have been here before. I have been here thousands of times and I will see the sign another thousand times. I have been here before. I have been here many times. All the wishing for death and the desperate, confused, scared, lost and burned echo's are nothing more than a child's game with the Creator. But at this moment, this is my death and I am not scared. I have committed every sin possible in my mind to justify the human race. I don't need that thought now. All I need is a warm blanket and a red mild kiss, and the red vibrating sign on the road side is God saying, "It's okay. I love you." I look up and I say I love you back with a heart that once was screaming with fury and contempt for a God that walks around dropping seeds and watching them grow. I stare at the red sign and it stares back. We play that game for a while. How long have I been sitting here? It could have been a year or it could have been just a moment. Nothing would surprise me.

I can't do this. I have to go. I drive away with a dull energy but with the only energy I can muster. Maybe I am not going to die tonight. Maybe I will make it through. I have to keep going. The star shows itself to me again and I follow like a magnet slowly being pulled closer. I think about the gypsy and realize that I have lost many battles with her. Maybe all this is in my head. Maybe she lives a peaceful life now with a peaceful man. I hope so because no one deserves a crazy psycho like me. I realize it is time to make my peace with her or my stalker delusion will be with me all my life. What life? Do I even have a life? Do I need to die? Will I die this night? Do I want to die? I turn music on and I realize that I am a sailor following a star home with a hope of someone that will be there for me. I finally realize that it has all been a dream and I can't wake up. Wake up! Toby, Wake Up! Keep going. She isn't here and never has been.

I look down at the gas gauge and realize I am below empty. There isn't a gas station anywhere around and I don't know what I am going to do. Gas stations aren't even open at 2 o'clock in the morning. Wait, you have to be kidding me. There is one. I pull into the station and realize it is only for trucks. I am freaking out. What am I going to do? I could go wake up one of the truckers and ask him for gas. Diesel? No. What am I going to do? I am going to end up on the side of the road somewhere stranded while death perches above me. Just get in your car and start going. Don't look back. Don't look at the star just look at the road and go fast. About two miles down the road there is a gas station. It is a miracle. I make it. The pumps are electronic so I can fill up with my card.

I get back in my car and start driving. I look back at the gas station and the lights give me the same feeling that the red light gave me. I am going to die. I realize this is the point where I stop being. I end. I end here. It will be death in a flash. Non-existence when I blink. I am here. I am gone. I will be nothing. I will not exist. I see it and it is pale and sharp and it will happen at any moment. However, a quick grave does not arrive only a sick man that has fallen and is pulling himself up. I am not gone. I am not dead. I am here and I don't feel bad. I have a second chance. I am continuing.

My belly is empty so I take a drink of water. I have been avoiding food and sleep for such long time. How long have I been lost in the machines? I have some water now. I do feel better. My mind is not split, but it feels hurt. My brain has been through too much and I just drive. I see a sign that says GLENWOOD SPRINGS, which means I have only three hours to go. I am going to make it home. Happiness grabs me and for a few minutes an honest life spins.

Out of nowhere the rocks start changing. The most beautiful hallucination I have ever seen is in front of me and it is so natural. The light that reflects off the rocks is molding them into weird shapes. There are rocks on both sides of me and maybe this is the end. They will cave in all around me. All the rocks are moving. It is the most beautiful thing I have ever seen. It reminds me of one of those mellow rides you take at Disneyland where things are around you to amaze you as you watch in a detached way. I keep driving and the rocks are turning and falling. This is so beautiful. Music is in the background and my eyes are like a starving child that finally gets a taste of food. It is so bright and I feel at peace finally.

My sexuality is charged because the machines are taking over. This is stronger than they have ever been. It is like everything around me is kissing me. Neon lights are everywhere and some of them are flashing by me while the others make pictures of leaves in front of me. What is going on? It isn't like before, it is pure. I see a huge power plant. There is no power plant in the middle of the Rockies. The power plant blows up clouds of smoke and the two clouds form two 'beings' that connect.

I keep going and the hallucination gets stronger. A man's face pops out in front of me. He is red and he tells me, "No!"

What was that?

I keep driving and the hallucinations stop and so do the machines. I take a right turn and realize I am on some strange road out in the middle of nowhere. I didn't take any exits and I should be on the highway. Am I on some random planet? I keep driving and realize that I have another chance in the world. I think I died by the red sign. Maybe this is heaven. It is so real. Where is this road going to lead? Where am I? I keep driving and think of being with some new random girl. I am not thinking of Diana. I keep driving and realize that it is the gypsy that I should be with. The red hallucination told me. The world looks new to me, almost like it is possible. The way she comes in and looks at me as if some secret will be revealed or maybe our bullshitting can go away and we can talk through the hallucinations. Do they know I hallucinate? Does anyone know I hallucinate? Gypsy! What a fucking crazy orgasm. Maybe I am going to heaven. Maybe I am already there.

The sign "GLENWOOD SPRINGS" pops up and I can't figure it out. How long have I been driving? How is it that I am seeing this again? Was that hallucination all in my head? I have to drive three more hours again?

The rest of the drive home is melancholy. I think my body has just had enough and I am not tripping my balls off but I feel okay. I think I was shown a different dimension for a short while. I make my way to Denver and stop in Golden. It is morning now, and I don't know how many days it's been since I've slept or eaten anything substantial.

Was that the gypsy? If we don't connect maybe I can find some other girl. I go into my coffee shop and I order some coffee. Lisa is there and she looks worried. About me? I bet Kelly told her I left town. Lisa looks worried but she sees that I look okay. I walk into the bathroom and look at my hair. It is curly but it looks good. My eyes have the same glimmer that my brother's eyes had. Did the machines do this? As I walk out the door I see Diana. She is with some friends and we talk for a little while. She is such a cool girl. I look good and have a swagger in my step. I think it's funny that I could take a trip to Vegas and back with no sleep and nothing to eat and still look halfway decent. No, I look good. I still have on my suit and how many times has the coffee shop crew seen me in my suit.

The gypsy has me hooked and I am stuck. I drive over to my mom's house to let her know I am okay. It is early and they all wake up. My mom tries to talk to me and wants to feed me but I need to sit. I go to the computer and find a chat room. Everyone is talking. The gypsy is there and she is telling me that she hates me. There is also a picture of a girl (the gypsy?) whose arms and shoulders look like mine. I am so skinny that you can see bones. I realize that I have been right all along and that she is going through the same hell I am. I can't do this to her. I get in my car and drive home. I walk upstairs and fall asleep. This kind of sleep is not sleep it's more like being dead. It feels so nice.

After about 16 hours of sleep I wake up and am feeling better. It is late in the day and I feel like walking as usual. The night starts winding down and I get this feeling that I have to choose between two different women. Their lives depend on it. There is the gypsy and there is Diana. The man at the car dealership said it would happen. He stated this in his backward talk and I don't want either of them to die. The sun comes up and I choose in my heart what is best and I choose the pagan gypsy. I can see her pain. I can see her and no matter what sins she has committed, I choose her. Love your enemy. As I watch the sun rise, hurt hits me. I have just killed Diana. It is so real. In my mind I have murdered her. My whole being aches. I feel a depression that is worse than death.

I know I can't get through it on my own. My mind is cracked and my soul has broken into pieces. The low is the lowest I have been. I know I need help. I go to my mom and tell her to put me in the hospital. I just don't care anymore about anything. I finally get to go there.

I relinquish control.

# 29
## Mental Hospital

**M**y mom and I walked into the hospital and I felt sick because somehow I knew the reality of where I was going. I could imagine steel bars on windows and straight jackets. We stepped up front to the secretary at the regular hospital and she took all my information. She told us to go sit in the lounge and wait. We sat down next to a guy whose hand had been cut and there was blood gushing from it. My mom made small talk but I sat quietly. About 15 minutes passed and they called my name.

*I can't wait to go to this hospital and heal wounds left by bad hallucinations and self absorbed delusions. My hands are a miracle though; I think I am a walking miracle. Will the outside machines still stay with me? Maybe I can help save the people in the hospital.*

We made our way into the interview room and my mom and I both sat down. This is the second time I have been in this seat at Lutheran hospital. *They didn't do shit when I punched myself in the face five times and they didn't do shit when*

*I took a piece of glass and cut a line through my heart. They will probably just let me go.*

*NO! I will help these people in here. I can't go back to being a crippled shadow. I have to go someplace else, someplace not in my head.*

The doctor is smug and my mom is doing all the talking. I am glad because I am fucking exhausted. A nurse comes in and takes my blood pressure and weight. I am standing bare footed on a white piece of plastic and it's cold.

The nurse says, "It looks like you weigh about 140 pounds."

I am calm and I show her how calm I am by smiling and saying, "That can't be right, I couldn't have lost that much weight. I weigh 190 pounds."

The nurse does not smile. She says, "No, you don't."

I look back at my mom and she does not look surprised. It makes sense, I guess. My only nourishment is smoke.

The doctor listens to the whole conversation and is attentive at this point.

He starts asking me questions but I don't feel like answering them. *His attitude makes him a cocky fuck, and I am not going to deal with these fucking therapists and shrinks anymore.*

*My mind is clear and I know where I am going. I have seen it in all the movies. The doctors forcing medication down your throat. Fuck this doctor and his demeanor. I will go into your shit hole and I will shut my ears to your dribble.*

The doctor says, "So, I have some questions for you, son."

I'm not his son! "Well, I don't feel like answering your questions."

The doctor doesn't look too surprised at my response. He says, "How come?"

I look at him and then I look at my poor mom and say, "Look, I am here for a reason this time. I can't take it anymore. I don't want to talk now. I just want you to make

all the confusion go away."

He asks, "Do you hear voices?"

And I say, "Kind of."

He asks, "Do you have hallucinations?"

And I say, "Yes."

He asks, "Do you feel like you have a strong desire to do amazing things?"

And I say, "Yes."

He asks, "Do you sleep every night?"

And I say, "No."

My mom speaks up now. "He has cut his chest, burned his feet, and punched himself in the face."

The doctor says, "Well, son, it looks like you need a little time to get things straightened out."

*I am just following orders now. They put me in an ambulance with two paramedics who happen to be mellow. The ambulance drives up to West Pines.*

*As the two paramedics take me by the arms and walk me through security they open two large doors which are the gate to whatever hell is in store for me. There is a nurse there to meet me.*

*The nurse greets me with, "Hello, Tobyn. Or is it Toby?"*

*I reply, "Doesn't matter." I say this because it doesn't matter.*

*I look around at this mental hospital and it isn't like the movies. It looks more like a giant lounge with couches, a TV and two hallways. There is a glass security window in the front and a large table that separates me from the nurses. There are a few people there. There is an old lady in a chair slipping down almost to the floor. I figure, hey, this isn't so bad; of course everyone is sleeping now. We will see what tomorrow has in store.*

*The nurse tells me that she has to take my picture and I have no problem with that. I normally hate photographs. I usually make funny faces and whoever is taking the picture gets pissed off. This picture I am more than happy to pose for. If they want a crazy man; they have got it.*

*The nurse takes the picture and asks me if I want to see it. She puts it in front of me. I am grinning like a fucking idiot and my hand is cupped on my chest.*

*The nurse gives me a little cup of pills and tells me where my room is located. She is sweet. It makes it easier. I am not going to sit on the couch. No, I am going to lie down. As I walk into my room, I see two beds.*

*I realize how alone I am in here. I have to face the demons alone and I am alone. I wonder if Kelly is worried about me. I wonder if my brother is worried about me. I wonder if Lisa is worried about me. I have caused so much pain and I have hurt people. I will just lie down on the bed. I wonder if the nurses and the doctors know what is in my head. They can't, but they do. They can all read my mind.*

*I pull the sheets up and I am surprised at how well they cover my head. A strong image is hovering over me. It is large and I can feel a strong man's presence. I don't say a word and I try to make him go away by putting my face in the pillow. He is big and he is yelling. He always yells at me. It's the same old stuff. He keeps up with his eternal yelling. I can feel his anger and I am pissed. I am freaked out but I am so tired of this shit. I am tired of the machines. The Ativan kicks in and my eyes feel slow.*

*The next morning is different. All the people are out in the open and I'm surprised at how many of them look normal. There is a kid that has all dark clothes and a weird hair cut. I look down at his belt and see that they took his belt away too. I guess a belt would make a good tool if you wanted to kill yourself. The rooms feel dirty. There is a filth that can't be described. Sort of like ten homeless guys coming into a place and having the party of the century. They have touched everything. I walk out and I see a heavyset girl with huge chunks of hair missing. She acts humble and you get the impression that she doesn't want anyone to see her. There is another girl that has red cheeks but looks normal.*

*I go over and sit on the couch next to an old man. He smiles at me and I smile back. I remember that maybe I can cure him by touching him. Jesus made miracles happen so why can't I. I reach out and put my hand on his shoulder. I ask him if he is okay. Touching him was good. The bones of his shoulder made me think* of rocks and stones. I guess when you sleep on rocks night after night you eventually find warmth in them. In the back of my mind I knew I wouldn't save anyone but I believed it might happen. The old man is my favorite person so far. His smile is a beacon of light that I can see. I ask him his name and he tells me it is George. I tell him it is nice to meet him.

The manic is here. I feel a strong desire to smoke and to walk; the same desire that has allowed me to come this far. The pacing begins and I move my way from one end of the hall to the other. Joy! Ecstasy! I feel at home again. I walk up to a nurse and ask her when I can have some cigarettes. She tells me, "Every hour."

I have a weird sensation after I take my meds. I feel itchy. It feels like my desire to move fast is pushing up against a wall, and I feel dirty. I smoke a cigarette and talk to a couple of people. We come back inside for group therapy. The lady in charge of Group says that we will meet three times a day. The last place I want to go is Group.

I am hungry and I want some food. I remember that there is cereal and milk and I go fix myself a bowl. The nurse said that the meds I am on will make me hungry.

Group meets again. It is what it is.

I decide to take a shower. I go into my bathroom and the Goddess (gypsy) pays me a visit in the floor. I can see her and she feels close but far away. She has been with me for so long, a dream, a delusion, a hallucination, the half of me that won't show itself. I feel her like I feel bone marrow. She wants me to dance. I stare into the yellow tiles. Fuck, I can't do this anymore. I need help and that's why I am here -- so leave me alone. I walk out the door and the same cold crippling feeling hits me. I feel like the black cloud is all over me again and is pushing me down. I see George as I make my way into the room and I go to him. He and I chat.

The next 6 days consist of a routine:
Day 1
Cigarettes every hour
3 groups
Cheerios and milk every 2 hours
Static that muffles my energy constantly

*Pacing*
*Brain having too many ideas*
*Eating too much*

*Day 2*
*Girl comes up to me and tells me I look like everyone in the world and then tries to give an old man a blow job.*

*Cigarettes every hour*
*3 groups*
*Cheerios and milk every 2 hours*
*Static that muffles my energy constantly*
*Pacing*
*Brain having too many ideas*
*Eating too much*

*Day 3*
*My mom shows up with my guitar and we sit on the couch. She tells me that she has been here to see me every day, but I don't remember seeing her. A random girl who had just been transferred into the unit comes over and is excited to see me play. I ask her if she plays and she tells me she does. I tell her that I would rather hear her play, so she plays. Her voice makes me feel like me. She has an eclectic thing about her but she is so sweet. She then hands me the guitar and I play her a few songs. Later that day she gets transferred and I am bummed about it.*

*Cigarettes every hour*
*3 groups*
*(During first group, the leader told us we were standing on our planet and we were supposed to pull ourselves away from the planet. We would be able to step back and see the earth as a whole. After the exercise I almost feel better.)*
*Cheerios and milk every 2 hours*
*Static that muffles my energy constantly*
*Pacing*
*Brain having too many ideas*
*Eating too much*

*Day 4*

*On day four I have had it. It is time to leave. The fence in the back is ridiculously tall and no one in their right mind would try to climb it. I think to myself, where will I go if I go over and I realize that I just want some fresh air. Air that a free man breathes. Not air that is regulated constantly where there is no sense of being a real person.*

*I am smoking a cigarette with the red cheeked girl. I toss my shoes over the fence and start climbing. She is freaking out. Oh well. I get to the top and am ready to jump and I turn back, look at her and say, "Bye-bye."*

*The first thing I do after hitting the ground is take a deep breath. Fuck that feels good. I start walking and I think, Now, where shall I go? I know. I will walk to C mart and call someone. The grass has soft sprinkles of snow on it and it is cold. I finally get there and stand next to the phone. Who should I call, Kelly, my brother, Lisa, Millie, my sister, my mom? Fuck, they all would tell me to go back. It is too cold out here anyway. I am going to go back and face this. It was so worth it just to get out of that place for a breath of fresh air."*

*The rest of the day...*

*They take my cigarettes away (They think I will go over the fence again.)*

> *3 groups*
> *Cheerios and Milk every 2 hours*
> *Static that muffles my energy constantly*
> *Pacing*
> *Brain having too many ideas*
> *Eating too much*

*At the end of the day Kelly visits and laughs at my escape attempt even though I don't tell him I just needed fresh air. My mom and brother are with him and we all talk. My mom tells me to please not try to escape again. The hospital called her at work and told her that I had jumped the fence and they didn't know where I was.*

*Kelly sort of takes me aside and gives me a hug. He tells me that Elliot Smith committed suicide. My jaw drops. I look at him* and say, "No fucking way!" He then realizes where he is and that it is dangerous to tell someone in a mental hospital that one of their favorite singer-songwriters has killed himself. I comfort him when he starts saying, "Sorry, sorry, sorry!" I tell him that it is okay that he told me. My brother walks over to us and hands me a book (such a typical brother thing to do). I realize that he doesn't know what to say to me. I give my mom a hug and assure her that I will not climb the fence again and then they are gone. It was exhausting for them to all come see me. I feel so responsible for all their discomfort. Now, I am off in my little paradise and have no idea when I am going to get out. I seem to be thinking clearer but these meds make me sleep so much. As I walk down the hallway, I throw my brother's book in a trash can. There is nothing symbolic about it. I just could not read it in a million years, not in this place.

An hour later my doctor visits me. He asks about my depression and my delusions I tell him that I'm depressed only because I'm in this place. He asks me if I still think I am the savior. I tell him I can't shake it and the idea is seeping out of my pores. I hate myself because of who I am. He then leaves the room and all my hopes are focused on an exit sign that hangs on the top of the locked door.

Day 5
I still don't have any cigarettes
3 groups
Cheerios and milk every 2 hours
Static that muffles my energy constantly
Pacing
Brain having too many ideas
Eating too much
In the middle of the day Millie and my sister stop by.

I am restless when they come. I fucking hate that they all have to see me like this but I love them for coming.

We are sitting together and Millie hands me a Rolling Stone magazine. I like Rolling Stone and I grab it. I start looking at the pictures and there are two picture pages of up-and-coming musicians. I look at it closely and they are all looking straight at me. Their eyes are open! They come to life. I can see them laughing at a musician that will never be. They have smirks on their faces and they all look perfect. I look at Millie and my sister and tell them to "get the fuck out of here." They leave with stricken looks on their faces. I walk into my room and start shadow boxing vigorously.

It is time for Group and Susan is there. She is about my age and seems cool. We are talking and listening. Anyone can hear what's in my head and Susan's nose looks like a pig's nose. I don't want to hurt anyone. She can hear me calling her names. Shut the fuck up, Toby. You're acting like a 3$^{rd}$ grader. I can't stop it. Just look away. Tell her you're sorry. Wait, she knows I am sorry because she can read my thoughts.

Day 6

Lorene, the heavier set girl whose hair is half gone, will not eat and she and I have become friends. When she tells everyone that she won't eat, I sit down next to her and explain how good she will feel after she eats. We have connected and I can feel her in my head reading my thoughts.

I still don't have any cigarettes

3 groups

Cheerios and milk every 2 hours

Static that muffles my energy constantly

Pacing

Brain having too many ideas

Eating too much

Day 7

It is time to go home and I am so relieved. This place has had its moments but it is frustrating too. George comes up to me and asks me if I am leaving. George has been a friend in all this. I think he and I have become close because we both smile at each other. We look each other in the eye. He is such a kind old man. He tells me that he doesn't know how he can get through it without me and I tell him that he will be just fine and kiss him on the cheek. He grabs my hand and we sit together. I can't understand why he isn't in an Alzheimer's unit or something. He isn't crazy, he is just old. He tells me again that he can't make it without me. I feel so bad because he is so lost. And he is so scared.

I also give my number to Loran who seems so lonely. I tell her that if she needs a friend to call and if she has no place to go for Thanksgiving, she is more than welcome to join our family.

My brother and mom meet with the doctor and assure him that they will be with me and I will be moving into my Mom's house. I am sitting here listening to the banter and the promises that they make to get me out of this awful place. Occasionally they look at me and ask me if I have anything to add and if all this makes sense to me. I assure them that it does and I will be just fine.

I am off. I still have some problems but my mind seems clearer now. The drug the doctor prescribes is Zyprexa. The doctor tells me that I am bipolar with schizoaffective disorder. The hallucinations, the delusions, the mania, the split brain, the wonderful highs and the horrid lows, the outside energy, the machines, the idea that I am a savior, and people knowing what I'm thinking are bipolar schizoaffective disorder symptoms.

No! Fuck that! I am not bipolar. I just had an episode because of my father's death and taking ecstasy. I am going to take the meds though. I almost feel back to normal but I sleep so much. Who cares anyway? I will take it till I am me again, and once my brain thinks clearly, I am off these meds. How did I get to this place? How could I get so low?

# 30

## The Order

The first day I got home from the hospital the mania was still strong and I felt a need to do something strange. I walked around my entire neighborhood doing a Charlie Chaplin imitation. Then I felt more on the straight and narrow. I took baths because it was calming. I also was on the computer quite a bit.

A few days after I got out of the hospital I felt relieved. By some miracle, the drug (Zyprexa) had worked. My mind was not going in two directions, the energy and the machines had all left me and I felt like my old self, kinda. There was a new thing plastered in my mind. Food! The drugs had some interesting side affects. I slept 16 hours a day and my feet felt like bones coming out of my skin when I was lying on the couch. I didn't like it but it was true relief to have peace of mind and to not want to walk constantly. I did occasionally get the urge and I did go for walks but there wasn't so much madness in it.

My independence had been stripped and I had two

(my mom and my sister) nurses who watched me closely. My passions had also been destroyed. That was what the meds did. So I mostly watched TV and played games on the computer. I played chess because my brother always beat me and I was looking forward to the day that I could stomp on him. He is such a bad loser and it would be so great to be able to beat him.

I had an appointment with the doctor and I had a lot of questions. They said that I was bi-polar with schizoaffective disorder and that I would have to be on meds all my life. The nurse practitioner was the one talking with me. She asked me if I had mood swings, which I did. She asked me if I thought that people knew what I was thinking. My answer was, "Yes, but you already knew that! You can read my mind. Really and truly, you don't have to ask me anything. Now do you?" She also asked me if I had grandiose ideas. I told her that I thought I was the savior or the false prophet. She told me that it was common for people to magnify their religious thoughts when they were bipolar with schizoaffective disorder. She kept asking me questions and my answers pointed to the fact that I was bipolar.

I still didn't believe it. My father died and I was mourning the loss. That was all. I think the doctors like to put labels on people just so they can treat with medications and feel like they know what they are doing. I didn't buy it and I told her that. She told me that most people with their first bipolar experience don't believe it. She started to talk about my medication and asked me if I was eating lots of sweets. She was reading my mind and knew that I had strong cravings for sweets. She told me I would gain weight. I weighed forty or fifty pounds under my normal weight so I figured it would do me some good. She asked me again if I thought that other people could hear my thoughts.

As I walked out the room I thought of how one day I would not be on the meds. My mom totally agreed with me. She didn't like them putting a label on me and agreed that

I was just having trouble because of unresolved issues I had with my dead father.

I spent time with Jayde. It was always fun playing with a five year old. She was so full of life and I was so lifeless.

I found myself missing the highs and lows even though they had hurt me. I saw patches of heaven back then and now I only saw a dull computer screen and had a dull existence. It gets better after a while and you don't feel so bland, so they said.

My mom asked me after a few weeks if I wanted to do some volunteering to get myself together. There was a need for volunteers at her agency with the refugees. I decided to do it. I felt like I could be productive in my search to find a balanced place after all the highs and lows.

The refugee building was modest. The secretary could barely speak English but I put on the "Tolini" charm to make her smile. It felt good to be myself and to consider someone other than myself. We talked for a little while and then I was introduced to the Director. He was an English guy and had a thick accent. The first day I sorted clothes from a huge storage unit. The clothes had that vintage Salvation Army smell to them but I was not afraid to get my hands dirty. I was sorting out gifts for people; people who needed the bare necessities of life. I could feel the Zyprexa in my system and my energy level was low, but I kept going.

The English Director stopped by and I hung out with him while he did his thing. We got back to the office and he told me what my new job would be. I was going to take refugees to their doctor appointments. My car was new and had snow tires and the job sounded awesome. I would get to actually be with these poor refugees who have waited years to come to our country. He told me I would start driving the next day. He gave me a list of people to transport and their addresses. I drove home excited. I didn't have to live in a world of making millions of dollars to save everyone. I could just do it one at a time.

When I got home I saw that my sister had been to the grocery store. She had bought this huge tub of ice cream. I went straight to the freezer and devoured it in minutes. It tasted so good. I had gone from forgetting to eat to sitting in a chair and basking in the glow of gorging myself. She was puzzled that I would eat all the ice cream and I didn't know what to tell her except that I had a crazy yearning to devour as many sweets as I could. She smiled and asked me to please save some of the cookies for Jayde.

I slept a sweet sleep knowing that in the morning I would be an asset, not a liability, to humanity. I knew the language barrier would be tough but I wanted to be a smiling face for people who had been through so much. The first guy I met was great. He was a short, black, bald man and his English was fair. The apartment complex he lived in was horrible but he had optimism that was incredible. He told me that one day he would own a car like mine and own a house. I thought to myself how hard it had been for me to even get interviews for a job and I had a marketing degree but.... maybe this man would get a chance. I had problems finding the doctor's office but I eventually did. I took him into the office and he got a check up. He told me how excited he was because he had met his first friend in America. I was pleased but not sure of his intentions. When we got back to his dumpy apartment he gave me his phone number and I gave him mine. Two days later I actually called him to see how things were going. I wanted to be a friend for him. I could barely understand him over the phone. We kept talking with the awkwardness of two people that couldn't connect. In the weeks ahead he called again but our friendship only lasted for a short time. I couldn't quite function as a friend yet and I couldn't understand him.

There were other people that I took to doctors' offices. One family stood out. I tried to talk and listen but they all had a look of terror on their faces. I didn't know if it was because of what they had gone through to get to

America or if it was me in my big fancy car, but I tried to respect them and not be too pushy.

I found myself driving around in circles. My two-way thinking was gone but now I was this foolish bland mule trying to move. I got lost everywhere I went and I realized that maybe the doctor was right and I was not ready to work. This job was an enlightening and interesting experience but my anxiety level was too much. I quit.

Now my days comprised of the computer and TV. What a waste I had become. At least I was not chasing white and the gypsy was a fantasy memory that made me realize how sick I was. I dreamt now of angel food cake, pecan pie, apple pie, birthday cakes, carrot cakes, cherry pies, cheesecake, chocolate cakes, M&M's, peach cobbler, key lime pie (so good), Butterfinger bars, Phish Food ice cream, brownies, chocolate donuts, glazed donuts, the donuts that have the sprinkles on them and my all time favorite, maple donuts. Every day I went out of my way to get a maple donut.

I started working at the coffee shop part time and it was hard. People didn't understand how a person who was so fast could now be so slow. It was the meds and most people didn't get it.

There was a new girl in my life, Christine. I was standing outside one day smoking and we started talking. I asked her for her number and we went on a hike for our first date. We seemed to hit it off. She was an art teacher and was striking. She had broken up with her boyfriend and I was sort of a rebound. I liked this girl and we had fun together. She made everything we did together fun and told me the most random things. We talked about art and she showed me things she had created. To actually touch someone instead of delusional touching was like a warm blanket on a cold night. To feel flesh and blood against me gave me peace of mind. It reminded me of the first day of spring when the aspens started getting leaves. These were the most intense feelings I'd had for a girl. One morning she was going on her usual run and she ran past the coffee shop. It was cute. We did all the normal couple things. We went downtown to the usual hang out and spent time hiding in the corner of Jazz bars all over Denver. One night at about two o'clock in the morning we went to Denny's and there was no one there. We spent time sneaking kisses and laughing. There was something in her eye that made me uneasy. It reminded me of the gypsy.

For some reason I didn't trust her. Months and months of dating turned sour. I didn't know what to say. If you can't trust someone, a relationship cannot work. So it ended.

I started an internship at a homeless shelter while I was working at the coffee shop. I had a pristine image of me hanging out with homeless people and just listening to them. Instead, with my marketing degree, I was put in the Public Relations Department. The meds made this difficult. I needed so much sleep that I had to drag myself to the shelter every day. I got there but I wasn't there. They had me reading the paper every day and although I could read it, it didn't seem to me to be helping homeless men and women. I wish I could have told them about the medicine, but I couldn't. It would be a reflection of my problems and people look down on someone who is drug dependent. I stayed there and I worked. I was in the corporate office and I didn't belong. A few months passed and I stopped working there. By this time I was weighing over 200 pounds. Amazing, before the hospital I weighed 140 pounds.

I missed the relationship I had with Christine. I should have stuck it out. She was cool. She did have cats though and I frigging hate cats. I am so allergic to them that I actually get violently sick.

I was sober, my mind was clear and it had been a year since my breakdown. I decided to go off my meds. You can't just go off them or you will freak out. You have to gradually go off them, which I did. I took my last pill and I was a free man. I was not worried but at the same time they say if you are bipolar, each time you have an episode it gets worse. I knew I was taking a chance.

Being drug free was nice. I wanted to lose all the weight I had gained but it took work. I worried that the machines would come back and I worried about what kind of creature I would become if they did come back.

# 31

## Gentle Street Walker

**F**ive months after I went off my meds I was still sane and generally happy. My father had been dead for a while and although I was still angry with him I had learned to forgive him. I didn't think about him all the time. I felt like I had taken my life back and my religious, fanatic days were gone. I had lost thirty pounds as soon as I quit the drugs and was back down to my normal weight. I felt like me again. But I was a man marked by stale memories.

The doctor told me that it was common for a person with bipolar to have the delusions that I'd had. Religion seemed to feed the bipolar delusions. I wanted to get a tattoo to remember those days and how I came out of it clean. I found a Celtic cross that symbolized the dead becoming like new. I got the tattoo to remember what it was like to be a child and to dream dreams. I got it on my calf. It was a weird place for a tattoo but it was a stepping stone for me. I could actually see myself living a normal life with normal impulses. There are reasons for everything and in my mind I was tested and failed.

I partied with friends and the nights were full of laughter, cynicism, listening, and ranting. We were pushing the limits of trying to do something good in the world and still fulfill our dreams. I was still working at the coffee shop but I also found a professional job. It paid well compared to my coffee job.

I still went on my walks. Walking still gave me peace. Who would have thought that in chaos and sobriety I could find peace. I thought about all of those walks I took when I was in chaos and the determination I had to run toward something and to find answers. I didn't just sit in my stuffy apartment and rot. I took action while I was sick. I could remember running hard to get the poison out while people would stare in bewilderment.

My new job was challenging. It was a mean job and could make any man depressed. Everyone says you should do what you love. They say that no one should be stuck in a job they don't like. Well, I would like to tell that person that if work was fun then it wouldn't be work. I worked downtown Denver; the place where dreams come true; the place where half the population is wealthy business men and the other half is the homeless begging for a dime. I was the wealthy business man with my nice business suit neatly pressed. I worked on Seventeenth Street in the 4-10 building on the tenth floor.

One day as I walked across the Sixteen Street Mall I saw a woman that was crippled beyond belief. She was in a wheel chair and could barely move her head. Her face had a horrible scar on it and it made me sick to look at her even after working with the homeless. I thought as I passed her that I would love to pick her up in my arms and just hold her. She looked so lost. I also thought to myself, "Could I end up being one of these pricks who walks right by her and doesn't care? I don't think so."

When I got to the office that day I ran into Jenny,

one of my associates and as we got on the elevator we greeted each other. We worked in the mortgage business trying to talk people into refinancing their home. She was the top salesperson, not because she had some amazing talent but mostly because she was attractive and the manager gave her all the leads.

My manager was a raging asshole. Day in and day out I heard, "Have you set an appointment yet today?" His mannerisms were manic and raging seemed to be his only joy in life. His screaming became an echo in my brain.

As Jenny and I walked into the office I heard the usual, 'how's it going?' from all of the other associates. Do they care? I ask myself. I sat down in front of my slow computer and looked at the leads for the day. Everyone showed up right on time and we had our usual morning meeting. Blah - blah - blah.

It was time to get on the phone and sell - sell - sell. I looked down at my feet and it was the only satisfaction that I knew I would get for the day. I always looked perfect except for my shoes. I wore these strange dress shoes (moccasins) that always put a smile on my face. They made me think about the mountain that I can see from my front yard. The mountain looks like a Native American who is going to jump up at any moment and come stomping across Denver on his rock legs. He's bigger than any of these man made buildings.

The guys I worked with, mostly retired lacrosse players, had an aggressive mentality. One of the guys bragged daily about how he spent a thousand dollars monthly on alcohol. I guess when everyone in the office is in their early twenties there is going to be a lot of drinking. I was by no means an exception to the rule.

That afternoon we all had to go to a presentation. The guys I rode with were good guys. They decided before we went to the presentation that we would all go to a strip club for lunch (like it's a casual thing). I wasn't hungry but these co-workers of mine were. They were eating big hunks of rare meat and watching nude women dance. I don't dig that kind of place. It just isn't my thing. I sat there and thought, this place is packed with guys watching these women sell a look at their bodies. They are selling to just anyone who has the cash. Judge not.

I thought it was funny how little everyone in the office knew about me. They didn't know about my father's death. They didn't know that I had a break down and ended up in a mental hospital. It had been a hard year for me but nothing that a week in a mild mannered mental institution can't cure.

Bipolar, no way!

The Doctors and their constant need to label people were hard to swallow. I will never forget the nurse saying, "Toby, you are bipolar." Well, I sure as hell didn't believe it. Yeah, I kept thinking, I spent a couple of months running around the mountains looking for something. But, look at me now. I am not there now. I haven't taken your bipolar schizoaffective meds for five months. I am doing just fine. I know. I know. I'm still a little screwy. The Pope died yesterday and when I saw the faces of those people in mourning it tweaked my brain a little. It's because they were so devastated over someone they didn't know. My father died a year ago and I still haven't cried. How could they get so upset about some Pope dying? I guess I'm callous. I just can't understand people running around downtown Denver weeping about the Pope's death.

Day after day, it was the same thing.

"Hey, Eric, how was that last call I made?"

"Good, Toby. You could have sounded more expressive though. You have to act like you have something that they are dying to have."

"I can't help it. I just have kind of a monotone voice." I thought, if only they could hear me when I am playing my music, I have been playing that stupid guitar for ten years and I know it's just a hobby but I also know that I'm not monotone.

"So, Toby, you should come out with us tonight," Danny asks me. He was the only lacrosse guy I liked. I always sang, "Danny Boy, the Pipes, the Pipes are calling." He got a kick out of it because he was Mexican and an Irish folk song wasn't quite a match.

"So, Toby, are you going out with us tonight?" asked Ralph. This was weird that both of these guys asked me to go out with them. I had never gone out with them before. They had also asked another guy, Mike.

Mike was my only real friend at work. He and I would actually do more than just bullshit. He was second in sales and had a stuttering problem. I think it was because people felt sorry for him so they would listen to him. I thought maybe I should start stuttering, it might boost my sales. Mike would probably be pissed. I could never do that him. It might work though.

That night we all ended up going from bar to bar. The lacrosse guys were fucking crazy. They kept buying me drink after drink. We ended up at a place called the 'Martini.' There were five of us. The lacrosse guys all talked a big game about hooking up with different girls but all of them clammed up the minute we walked into the club. I was not afraid of girls. I was a good looking Italian guy with a sharp wit and a good smile. I walked over to a table that was filled with 'Barbies' and I sat down and started talking to them. They, of course, responded with giggles and smiles and shallow remarks. Enough! I just couldn't do this. I got up and said, "Bye, bye, girls." The lacrosse guys were amazed. By this time the alcohol had sunk in and I was wasted. Now, you can have a buzz or you can be drunk or you can get wasted. I was definitely wasted. After talking briefly with Mike I told him that I had to go and I would see him tomorrow.

As I was walking out of the 'Martini' I thought it would be funny to stick my finger in my nose. These people were not my kind of people and never would be. I just loved looking back at the 'Barbies' with my finger in my nose and seeing the expression on their faces. Is this manic behavior? I wonder.

I started walking down the streets of downtown Denver and I started singing. "Oh Danny Boy, the Pipes the Pipes are calling." I sounded like the typical drunk Irish man. I kept singing it over and over. I'm glad I didn't run into a cop because I would have been arrested for drunk and disorderly conduct. "Oh Danny boy, the pipes the pipes are calling." My last name is Tolini, the kind of name that when people hear it, they get hungry for Italian food but I was half Irish and I loved that song.

When I am drunk like that, I always seek out and talk to homeless men. I'd interned at the homeless shelter and I had actually seen some rough things. I had also gone nuts a year ago and I could relate to the mentally ill. I felt more comfortable with the homeless bums than I did with a bar full of yuppies.

I saw a homeless guy standing in front of Walgreens on the Sixteenth Street Mall. He was a big guy and I asked him how he was doing. He said fine and walked away. He didn't even ask me for change. Oh well, maybe he wasn't homeless. I wasn't going to take the bus that charged down the Mall, because I needed to walk off the booze. I kept walking. An old tired looking African American stopped me looking for change. His skin was wrinkled probably because he had been out in the sun so much and his eyes had a strong red glaze around the pupil. All I could see was his face because it was cold outside and he was wearing many layers of clothing. I gave him five cigarettes and some change I had. We started talking and I sat down on the cold cement in my suit. He was quite the talker. We started talking about spiritual stuff and how society is so messed up. He then broke out about the machines and how they controlled him. I listened to him because I knew sometimes people just need to talk. He then started telling me how he had looked for a job and how hard it was to keep a job because he liked alcohol. I don't judge people. I mean everyone judges everyone all the time but I try to look past the muddy stuff and look at people in the eye. I told him about some of the mental issues I had and issues I had with my dead father. It is amazing how someone you don't know can shed light on a subject with an abstract point of view and how you can hear that point of view even though a dozen other people have already voiced it. He basically told me you have to forgive him now even though he is dead and if you don't you will never find peace. I was impressed with his wisdom and I had made a new friend. He introduced himself to me and I told him my name. I asked him if he needed a ride home or to a shelter and he said he would love that.

We started walking to my car and the first thing he noticed was a broken side window on my car. I told him that someone shot a BB through it and he said, "Man it sucks that people can have no respect." I was a little embarrassed to be driving such a nice car and glad that the window was broken. He told that me that he liked the car. At this point I was still drunk but, screw it, why not go get some food. Food always absorbs the liquor. I had the perfect place to go.

As we walked in, we were welcomed by some strange looks from the people in the diner. Here I was in a white shirt and tie and a tailored suit and an old homeless guy was my companion. I tried to find a seat where I wouldn't have to look at people, where I could just talk with my new friend. But truth hit me and I felt special because I was doing something for a homeless guy. I hated that I felt this way. I wished there had been no one but him and me in the Diner.

I ordered the chicken fried steak and he ordered water. I could see in his eyes how he wanted me to respect him and I wanted him to know that I did. I ordered the largest thing on the menu. My new friend kept talking about the machines and how they controlled him and he couldn't make them go away. He didn't know but I understood about the machines. They controlled me and it was not fun. I just listened.

I kept looking at his hands. They were huge compared to a normal man's hands. His hands reminded me of my Grandpa who had died six months before my father.

My Grandpa Tolini was such a man. The way a man should be. My Grandpa was cornered by a bull once and the only thing he could do was punch his way out of it. My Grandpa squared up and hit this bull right between the eyes. Obviously his hand was broken but the old bull backed off. Grandpa never got it fixed so he had one hand that was bigger than the other. His hands had scars all over them and his nails were never clean. My Grandpa, without a doubt, had working mans' hands.

I had found a man who had hands like the grand old man. I kept looking at the hands and observed that my new friend's hands were large but not in the same way as my Grandpa's. My new friend's hands looked like silky leather and had a lizard like quality to them. I assumed it was from years and years of sitting in the cold. I wanted to hold his hands and tell him everything will be all right. But everything will not be all right and this man was fighting demons that I had known and was familiar with.

Our meals came. One glass of water and one chicken fried steak. I started going to town because after about ten or so drinks you need greasy food. I got toast and I told the homeless man that I didn't like toast and he could have it if he wanted. I didn't want him to feel like he was homeless. I wanted him to feel like he was a friend. I finished about half of my plate of chicken fried steak. I told him that he could have it if he wanted it because I wasn't hungry enough to eat it all. Being the stereotypical American I could have eaten it all in one sitting but I wanted him to be able to maintain his pride and still get some food. He ate it with vigorous intent and I got my dose of being a 'kind' person.

I had spent a wonderful night with this gentle street

walker. I was so much more comfortable with him than I had been with the guys from my work. I felt like I had touched something real. As I was taking him to the shelter he gave me a card and said he could fix my car. I told him, that would be awesome and that I would call him. Just before he stepped out of the car, he said, "Who knows, Toby, you and I don't have a female right now but maybe one day when you get a girl and I get a girl, we could go out together." It was a sincere invitation that he was extending to me because he had nothing else to offer. I looked at him in the eye and said, "That would be nice." He smiled and left.

I made it home okay swerving away from the lines on the road. I took the card he gave me and put it on the dresser at the foot of my bed. When I looked close at the card I noticed there was a beautiful woman on one side of the card and a giant demon on the other side. I thought of his machines.

The next day I decided to call my new friend. No one answered. I left a message. The whole day was dull. I thought about the Pope dying. My brain felt like it was breaking. It had been five months without meds for me and I was proud that I had finally licked the bipolar stuff. I went to bed late because I was playing the guitar. I closed my eyes softly.

*I wake up in a state of horror. My eyes are open but my body cannot move. I have had this sensation before many times. It's awful because I am totally paralyzed. My body is still asleep but my mind isn't. There is something different this time. I see a six foot tall, four foot wide, blue neon circle at the end of my bead. There is a giant woman's face inside the circle. This thing is huge. She is screaming at me but I can't hear a word she is saying. This is a full-on hallucination. Her hue is bright and her face is vivid and real. She is beautiful and she is screaming at me with so much anger that I know she wants to kill me. I can't move. Frantically, I start to make myself move in my mind. I can feel her energy of hate but I put my head down so I can sleep. If I sleep she will go away. She keeps screaming and screaming. I can't figure out why she is so mad. She keeps screaming and screaming. I can't stop her. There is wind that keeps blowing across her blue face. I feel like she is justified by screaming at me, so I'm sorry. She keeps screaming and then she screams some more. Her mouth is moving so fast and her anger is unbridled. After feeling this destructive anger and realizing that she is not going to go away, I think to myself, no more. I start to come alive. I am not going to let this beautiful woman push on me with her anger. I am not going to let this beautiful woman destroy me. I raise my hand and I look at the hatred and I put my hand around her head and squeeze the beautiful hallucination into oblivion.*

*I'm stunned by what just happened. I'm horrified that I have killed someone. I go to the kitchen and I feel a thin line of dirt covering my whole body. I am not going to let the machines take me -- and fuck that homeless guy with his card. I have met men in my past that spill out poison and this old guy, no matter how humble he was, will not do it to me -- like Dan, the messenger, or the gypsy. I have had experience with evil and I am not going to allow it in again. I take the card and burn it. It is an omen to the man that I will not have bad spirits take hold of me. I burn all of it.*

*As I sit there and look at the ashes and think about how I need to bury them in the backyard,* it occurs to me, I could be in trouble. The delusions are starting again and my mind is not right. Where will they take me this time?

# 32

## Quiet Giant

**M**onday I was back at work. I didn't have "IT" full blown like I did before but I did have the strong desire to walk. I was at work, but I was not at work. My mind was lost in my dreams, but I was able to make phone calls to customers.

I got an hour lunch every day. Working downtown I saw things that inspired me. I spent my hour, not hanging out with the guys, but in coffee shops and restaurants writing poetry and songs. I had music in my head. I could do it without my guitar. It was easy to write lyrics when I had the music in my head. I had a strong feeling that I could save the world again. It wasn't by destroying Las Vegas; it was by writing small poems. I thought the reason we were in the state we were in was because no one was willing to learn about all the religions of the world and listen to people and experience different cultures. We have ambassadors but do we have people with foreign policy that know the culture so well that they can truly respect the culture? Wars could end.

If two people in a position of authority came together with a true desire to listen and they were able to bend their own ideas, imagine how peaceful everyone would be.

Maybe this already existed but I wanted to learn more. I wanted to respect the things I normally did not care about. My madness was in this and I read a book that describes world religion with conviction. It was a starting place for me. I knew there was much to learn but if I could only get a flavor for each 'herb,' maybe I could change the world. My obsession was found in a book again.

Day by day, when I was on my break at lunch, I wrote random ideas down and I wrote letters of respect. My mania was getting worse and I didn't know what to do with it. I wrote random poems that didn't mean much. The sad part was that I couldn't experience each religion in a real way. I wanted to respect each culture. I was sure that all I would do was offend. The struggle went on and on -- Writing and erasing and writing and erasing. The Christians say that the body of Christ is in each person and the prophecy of Him coming back can only be fulfilled if people develop. The body -- the bride. Maybe the 10 commandments are something to use as a guide. Maybe the five pillars show us discipline. Maybe the Hindu and Buddhist religion is the path to enlightenment, a way to see heaven on earth. Ying and Yang. Could the combinations be men and women in Paradise? A mixing bowl of religions could make something wonderful for all men's palate. A fool's thought.

**Tribes**
All these tribes
Each one with its own voice.
Church tribes, gang tribes
Corporate tribes, homeless tribes
Forgotten tribes, Police tribes.
Face to face at one another
Can you see you in me?

Can I see me in you?
Knives of ugly, guns of ambush.
Fair fights still lose.
Eye for an eye makes bad choice.
Lets all be blind,
And fused.
Anarchy

**Trying**

Trying so hard to complete a sentence.
The meds I have taken, burn with poison.
But other people make me swallow, Is it a gift?
They make me swallow the pills whole.
The pills make me feel like I'm crawling out of my skin
They make my speech slurred but my doctor says,
You have a disease.
I don't see it that way; I see it as a small thing I have to do.
I see it as a means to forget the delusions.
Drink up more fish oil and balance is near
Will I take the pills? I would rather break mirrors.

**Split**

Split in the seams of black and white.
Split in wrong or right.
Split and set to only one side,
Can't I look at the other? Can't I
Sit on that side?
We were all born on an edge somewhere.
We were all born on the edge of something.
I can't see you, you have gone too far.
On the edge I sit with a dull star.

**Muttle**
**Muttle**
**Muttle**

I want to learn. I have been so stuck in my little life that I am tired of hearing the same plot, the same words, the same goals, the same end.

The Native American mountain that I can see from my front yard is going to rise up. When I get home I see this giant figure breaking his mold and coming out of the mountains. I can see him running toward me and it is so vivid that I know the hallucinations are back. I can see him. He stands for absolute justice and his giant rock feet are going to stomp me because of my lack of respect.

My mind is wandering as I drive to work. Is this Monday? I see Diana's car parked in front of a building and all the same delusions seem to come back. I see the gypsy too. Stop the car! It might get towed. I don't care. I walk inside the building because the desire to see Diana is strong. I walk around in the building and realize that she is not here. Someone else has the same car. I get in my car and for a moment reality flashes but then the traffic light flashes green and my eyes are hypnotized. I have to follow it. I have to follow the lights. I keep going without looking back. I don't care if I'm late for work. I twist around downtown Denver until I see the clock on my dash. There is a boss yelling at me in the clock. I don't like the job and I think the company is telling the little people lies so if I get fired, oh well. I walk into the office and the boss isn't even there. The boss comes in a few minutes after I have arrived and we all get together in a group. The boss asks me a simple question. I don't know what to say. My mind is going one hundred miles an hour but I can't answer this simple question. The boss looks at me and asks me, "You all right?" Like I'm an idiot. I am familiar with being treated like a moron because of the poison. It doesn't bother me.

As I am sitting there with the group, a hallucination hits. Superman is flying around the building and pointing at me with anger. It happens over and over. I then see Jesus with clouds around him pointing at me. I just sit there and stare at him while he points. I am totally freaked out and want to get out of this place. I visualize myself running to the door and never looking back. The hallucination stops, thank God, but then I see a man in a building across the street wearing a white shirt. He is just standing there. Is this a hallucination? I can't make out any features except the white shirt. It is me standing there. I think it is my potential. It is my own energy standing there looking at me. I can feel myself in it. I sit there and look at my machine. There is strength in me standing there. Before I know it I find myself wanting to crawl underneath the desk because I am frightened at this mirror image. I am scared at what I might become. There is a silent power in the man.

Muttle
Muttle
Muttle

Lunch time and I have shaken off all these images. I am having a cigarette with my boss and a secretary. They finish their cigarettes and go back into the building. I look at the giant skyscrapers and I see the Native American mountain walking through them. I shutter and fall against the wall looking at him. He has the power to destroy every building and is justified because of things done to him in the past, but he doesn't. He is a calm, quiet giant. There is wisdom seeping from this hallucination. He is at peace. I shout at him, "I need peace -- your peace."

I have the same strong urge to run. I have to run the poison out. I start running (in my business suit) and my feet suddenly feel like they are lifting up. Could I fly? I stop immediately and wonder what world I am in. The delusions are worse and I can't take it. I get my car and drive home. Tomorrow is Friday and I will have the whole weekend to wander around the woods aimlessly.

The new day dawns. It's Friday. I get up. I didn't sleep much because I read the religion book all night. The depression hasn't hit me yet but I realize I might be sick in the head like that fucking nurse told me. I put Jimi Hendrix in my CD player as I drive to work. What an amazing man. I listen to the line, "... business man walking down the street pointing your plastic finger at me."

The words hit me. My dream is to be a musician like JH and here I am stuck in this horror of a job not doing what I want to do. I can see Jimi to the right of me and he is pointing his finger at me. So----I am walking down the middle of the Sixteenth Street Mall pointing my finger at him and saying, "Artist walking down the street pointing your finger at me." Or is he saying,"Business man walking down the street pointing your plastic finger at me?" I say it back to him. "Artist walking down the street pointing your finger at me." There is no anger, only my dreams blowing up like a pin sticking in a balloon.

Work is a muttle. I don't get fired so I must be working.

When I get home, I avoid my mom as much as possible. I know that she will see my mania and want to interfere with my plans. As I leave the house, she questions me and won't let me have the keys to my car. Maybe she does see it. I hate that she knows that I am like this because it causes so much pain.

As I am walking I discover a jackpot. I find a lake

close to my mom's house. I have to cross some barb wire, but I am psyched. The lake is close to the house and I sit and just stare at how amazing it is. I am so at peace for that moment and then there is total confusion. I hear someone yelling and running and as I turn around four or five police officers with guns pointed at my head tell me to put my hands in the air. In that moment the mania I have, multiplies many times over. I am just sitting by a lake, peaceful and happy, and these gun hungry crazy cops decide to show me what they have. I have a dick too. The rebellious nature in me explodes. I'm not going to jail easily. If I cooperate I probably won't go to jail but I am so pissed and out of touch with reality that I don't care.

The cops pull me over to their police car and start asking questions. They ask me where I live and I look at them and say, "Right here. I live on this spot of tar." I stick to my story and they get frustrated.

Then a cop asks what my name is. I tell him, "My name is Kunta Kinte." This is my own little private joke with myself because my name is Toby.

I am laughing and the cops don't think it is funny. They cuff me and put me in the back of the police car. As I am sitting there, I hear my cousin's voice in the trunk of the police car. I don't know what to do. I am so confined by these handcuffs behind my back. I am freaking out. I tell the cops to open the trunk and let my cousin out. I kick the back of the front seat over and over and I scream at the two cops in the front seat to let my cousin out of the trunk. I tell them that I will kick until we arrive at the police station if they don't let him out. He is my favorite cousin and I would die for him. When they pull me out at the police station, I look the officer in the eye and tell him he had better take my cousin out of the trunk. I can hear laughter behind me. A group of cops standing around are laughing their asses off. It doesn't shake me the tiniest bit.

They book me and put me in a cell. I start running

around in circles in the cell. It is funny to me. I run as fast as I can until my legs give out and I fly across the room. A police officer tells me in a decent way that I am going to hurt myself, so I stop. I notice a beautiful girl watching and I am not sure why she is here. Two years ago I would have acted prim and proper but I don't care. I start running around in circles again.

The cops think I am on drugs and they call an ambulance to take me to the hospital to draw blood. "Well, they won't find drugs in me. I'm just a freak."
Muttle
Muttle
Muttle

My mom meets me at the hospital. She heard the sirens and went to the police station first to tell them I am bipolar.

My brain is twisted.
I can't be here.
I start laughing. I start crying. I am yelling but none of the words make sense.

They put me in the ER and I have to wait while they do a drug test on me. I am totally gone while I am waiting. I think of a musician that does pot and for some reason I feel stoned. I start laughing, but eventually the real world hits me. I am talking and mumbling and screaming. I have totally lost it.

I hear a voice saying, "Give him some Ativan, NOW!" It sounds like my mom.

I am sitting on the floor screaming for the machines to leave.

I have completely lost it. This is the furthest my mind has ever stretched.

The machines are pulsing around me. These machines are monsters and I can see them vividly. I want them to go away but I don't know how to get rid of them. I take the sheet of my bed off and cover myself so I don't see the monsters. I am screaming for them to leave me alone.

The cops that pointed their guns at me started this.

Some nurse is on the floor with me and he is putting a needle in...

Muttle

Muttle

Muttle

I am in an ambulance again.

I feel better. Must be the meds.

This guy is talking to me. Sure I can talk. We are talking and he is taking my blood pressure. I'll bet it's off the charts. I laugh inside.

I feel peaceful. I have to trust in this modern medicine. But it's more than that. I can see a perfect medical system someday and it takes care of humanity but how can I live with all these scars.

We pull up to the mental hospital. I'm lost.

Muttle

Muttle

Muttle

# 33

## Mental Hospital Revisited

The doctors give me medication.

"Caleb, I can't believe how orange your shirt is. It is beautiful. You look good."

The next memory I have is my roommate who is standing ten feet away from the window staring at it. He won't move and I try to talk to him.

I go out of my room and look at the people in this place and am in shock at how much harder this ward is than the last ward I was on. My mom comes to visit me and she tells me that I have been there for more than three days. I don't remember any of those days. I guess one of my roommates was scary and he stole my jello. My mom was in the room and I screamed at the guy to give it back. She was in shock that I could be so hard but for the life of me I can't remember it. She leaves with tears in her eyes. I hate it when I make her cry. With her soft heart and all these crazy people walking around in here, maybe she is crying for all of us. Walking is a necessity because of the drugs they're giving me so I join in the parade. I find myself pacing back and forth from one end to the other, staring at the carpet. There are others pacing with me. If only I had the stretch of pavement that I had in Golden. I dream of sandy beaches. I squeeze my toes.

The drugs I'm on make me twitchy. The drugs I took before made me want to eat all the time but these make me eat one bite of food and leave a full plate behind. This place is filthy and I refuse to take a shower until I get my flip-flops. I got athletes foot the last time and I don't want to get that malady again.

This place is wall to wall sadistic. There is an anger and a desperation here that I don't want to see. Depravity exists and I am a part of it. I pass other people and we somehow are connected in this fast pacing marathon. They have the same raw intensity that I have.

When will I get out of here?

I can't do it anymore.

I can't take the illness when the answer to it is poison. I have to trade one poison for another.

The TV is slow in here. It reflects a life I will never have. Do I want it anyway? I just want to be on the road. I don't feel low being here (societal standards). I do feel real.

They don't know. The 'plastics' don't know. They don't know what it feels like to drown in a pool of tar and try to pull yourself out.

The phone has a telephone cord and the orderlies are not paying attention so I grab the cord and head for a room. My days are over in this world and I am too tired to even care anymore. I know that I can't help all the people I once thought I could help. I can't even help myself. The wall that I am facing is solid brick and I can't get through it.

I grab a chair and stand under the fan. I pull on it to see if it will hold me. It does. I tie the telephone cord around it and then start to tie it so my head will fit. I tell Jayde that I am sorry and that I love her. Laughter starts coming out of me.

When you are pushed as far as I am, laughter comes because you don't have to deal with it anymore and the end is close. I hold the cord and I tell God: "If you want something else for me you better stop this." There I go, testing God again. As I stand there laughing I visualize my death. I see it. I am sadistically happy with my laughter but I am melancholic to leave everyone behind. I start to put the cord around my neck and a girl walks in the room. The confusion on her face is enough to make me laugh harder. Here I am, a man trying to kill himself, laughing his fool head off. When she looks at me I start shaking and my laughter turns to tears because I can't do this anymore.

I guess God wants me here for something after all. The orderlies take me off the stool, take all the phone cords off the unit and make me sleep in the lobby every night so they can watch me. I can't even pee with the door closed.

The doctor walks in to ask me his psycho-babble questions. The first question he asks me is, "Toby, what is your depression level?"

I tell him, "Pretty high considering I just tried to kill myself."

"Yes, I heard about that. Why would you do that?"

"Doctor R., I just can't do it anymore--the whole bipolar thing."

The doctor looks at me and asks, "Do you feel suicidal now?"

"No."

The doctor asks me, "Are you still having delusions about being the savior or the false prophet?"

"Yes," I answer, "I just can't shake it off."

"Well, Toby, we have you on some medication that will help you."

"I don't feel right. It makes me feel jittery all over."

"That will go away, Toby. Do you have anxiety?"

"Yes, my anxiety is… I feel shaky."

The doctor looks away from me and says, "Well,

Toby, we are going to try to get you out of here soon if you behave."

"Doctor, I feel like I could do better at home. I know I am on new meds but I would do much better at home."

"No, Toby, We are going to keep you for a few more days."

Panic engulfs me. I have to be here locked up in this hell hole for who knows how many more days.

Days pass and I can't remember them. It's the same hospital but a different unit. My roommate still stands in one place all day. His name is Gabriel and I have to call a nurse because one day he has a seizure. My mom visits me every day and after several days asks me what I remember. I tell her about the ride to the hospital. "Oh yeah, Mom, when they were bringing me over here I knew that I could trust modern medicine because the EMT guy showed me it."

The days turn in this place and the medicine they give me makes me sicker and sicker. Everyone keeps pacing which is what I do too. I feel a sickness in this place and I want out. I don't want the bipolar anymore and I don't want constant medication.

I quit smoking in the hospital. The first day after the suicide attempt they wouldn't let me smoke, so when they told me I could, I said I didn't want to.

A man tries to punch me because he gave me some math equation and I gave it to the nurse. He is not happy with me and I have made a true enemy in this place.

I also made a few friends. One guy had a Bible he was reading constantly. He looked like a homeless guy but I don't know if he was. One day he came up to me and said, "I have it figured out." At this point I am tired of the religious banter, but I listen to him. He has this strange drawing and starts saying how it is the key to the sign of the beast. He tells me there are houses that make up 666. They are in a circle and on the outside are rectangular cubes. He then tells me everyone in a house and everyone in a hut and everyone on the street have the beast already imprinted on them because of sin. So I ask if he is the antichrist. He replies that anyone who doesn't "believe" is the antichrist. I am tired of this conversation and it hurts my head. I walk away slowly from the conversation because I don't know what the hell he is talking about. He and I still become friends.

My mom brings my harmonica and while the antichrist guy is smoking I play for him. He says he enjoys it and I am glad. I am glad to be able to give this man a little enjoyment.

My friends and family all visit. My mom comes straight from work everyday and the nurses let her in before visiting hours start because they can see how she calms me. It is nice. I see Lisa and her warm heart makes me almost run to her for a hug. I hate for them to see me like this and I tell my mom that I don't want them to come visit me. She lets them come though and it is good for me.

After two weeks my time was done, I had gotten so used to the place that I was afraid to go out in the real world. The doctor had found the right "cocktail" of meds for me and I was supposedly stable. I had done my share of pacing. My friend Kelly gave me a MP3 player which made the time go fast as I sat in the corner listening to it trying to forget where I was with my eyes closed and the medicine pulsing through my body. I wondered if I would recover. I knew that I was NOT normal and if I wasn't normal then I was still sick. I didn't indicate this to anyone -- but I knew. I did recover once but the delusions were worse this time and the medicine they gave me was making me sick.

I tried to meditate in this place but found no peace. My brain was moving too fast. I don't think anyone could find peace in a place like this.

The horror show in this unit compared to the other unit was black and white. There was a dirty film that covered the lining of this mental institution.

I met this cute girl, Abby, who came in for the last

five days of my stay. She had some serious problems but for some reason she was a comfort in this place. We talked and listened to each other babbling. She came from the streets and I compared her story with mine. At one point we almost hooked up in there just out of boredom.

I was dying to leave there. There was an old man (not George) who should have been in a nursing home and was filthy. He sat in the middle of the unit and I couldn't understand why they wouldn't wash his feet. Thank God for Abby. She got me through the last hard days.

In the first stay at West Pines there was Group three times a day where everyone talked and such, but this place was a free for all.

Finally they released me. I had tried to kill myself and they trusted me not to do it again. They were so clueless. If things got unbearable I had a perfect plan. I remembered feeling so complete when I knew it was the right thing to do. I guess someone can be pushed that far. I thought of leaving poor little Jayde behind and I realized I had to live for her.

I was glad to get home and I wanted to find a place where I could be myself and be excited for rain to fall, and be just as excited when the sun showed itself. I knew what I was facing and I hoped I could find myself again. I was a seed that could see everything I was doing and because it felt like a new start, I thought I might blossom. But there was still something that told me that I didn't have it yet. The drugs that they gave me took my will and I was fighting a never ending battle. I had to be on these things for the rest of my life. I had to get hold of it. I wanted to be on the meds because I realized I was bipolar schizoaffective and the meds would stop the delusions. Would that stop the hallucinations? Will the meds stop me from being led somewhere because it feels right? I had such conviction going to Las Vegas so long ago. How can I stop my convictions? Would the meds help me? Time would tell.

# 34
## Prison

Chapter 34
Prison

**M**y family had to move again a few days after I got home. The meds were too expensive for us to be able to live the way we were living. Everything was slow and blurry and I had a new malady. I was hearing voices. It's hard to explain. You don't actually hear voices through your ears. It is a muttle in your brain and the voices are buzzing around without control. I heard voices mostly from the gypsy and the Pop Star but I still heard the voices of other people. It was almost like having a conversation in your head all the time. There was no release and there was no stopping it. I wondered if the meds I was taking would take care of this eventually. The doctor I saw after my first trip to the mental hospital was right. Every time you go off the meds a break down is worse. This was when I knew I was a madman.

When it came time for moving day there were more

than ten guys to help move. I was a vegetable because of the meds. Moving day I just stood and watched. I felt bad but what could I do? We were moving from a beautiful house to a cinder block house. Our new house was the closest I have ever been to poverty. There were, however, good trails for walking or riding a bike in the neighborhood which led to a big field. The field wasn't grass but had shrubbery that you could walk around in. So I tried to look at the positives. The trails ran through the neighborhood and the houses were backed up to them. You could see the backyard of all the houses. There were dogs barking through fences as you passed by the houses. The further you went up the trail the more rural it became and then the trail ran for five miles through the foliage and trees.

The time I spent in the new house was a hell that I would never wish upon anyone. The person who lived there before had plastered red paint on the cinderblocks in the basement and because of my new persona it felt like blood was everywhere. Someone also painted 'redrum' in the bathroom. It was sadistic and twisted. It felt like the people who were there before us were horrific. My room was downstairs and I couldn't shake the red.

*The medicine I take makes me have hallucinations and I feel like a heroin addict trying to kick the habit. I don't know what that feels like but I know that the way I feel is completely unnatural. Basically my body is trying to get out of my skin and I can't stand up, sit down, lay down, pace, or walk around, which means I can't be anywhere. When I am in one of my peak times, I actually ask my mom to kill me. She sits with me all night as I jerk and moan and beg. I stop taking that medication the next day because the doctor says I have akathisia and I can't tolerate that med. I get on some other stuff but the hallucinations and the voices stay with me. When I am driving at night there are neon lights flying like dozens of shooting stars. There is an anxiety which makes it almost unbearable. I try to not drive at night but my friends want to see me. They don't know how crazy I still am. I should win an Oscar for my portrayal of a sane man.*

*Today Millie took me to a lake by my house and I almost felt at home. She brought such warmth with her. Her heart felt concern for me.*

*After getting off those sick meds I find a new freedom. My mom and sister watch me like a hawk but I find myself going where I want to go. I stand around our backyard and watch and wait for new hallucinations. I have one that sticks with me. I can see my friend Dustin drowning in mud. He is hurting and I don't know what to do about it. I go for walks and the images of him are so striking.*

*I know what I have to do. I have to get another tattoo. I know the one I need to get. By hurting myself, I will help Dustin. I get in my car and start driving. I drive like a race car driver because I want to stop my friend from hurting. I walk into the big tattoo shop and I tell the artist that I want a tattoo of the Sudanese flag on my arm.*

*I just want to stop their hurt.*

You would think by now that the reality of my delusions would be strong enough to stop me from getting the tattoo. You would think by now that logic would override delusion. The problem is that the signs are so strong that I have to follow my gut. I got the tattoo. Sudan represented the same turmoil that I felt in my own life. I saw visions and omens everywhere. *The voices in my head lead me to places that show me how close I am to God. It feels like He is reaching out to me. I know I can't live without meds and I keep taking them but I also keep holding on to my delusions like they are real.*

*When I come home and show my sister and my mom the tattoo, they are mortified. Their reaction makes me feel a dread.*

*The days keep passing and I still wonder if the voices will go away. I follow where they lead. I have taken time off work so I have time to heal. On a mediocre day I find myself in a deep depression. I am lying on the couch in the afternoon hoping to find myself. I am watching TV thinking about my future. I am watching the news and a politician comes on trying to gain votes for his candidacy. He starts talking about crime and connects mental illness with crime.*

*He is talking about gun control and says he wants to keep track of the mentally ill and criminals in order to control crime… like it is only the mentally ill that partake in crime. Sure there is a percentage of the mentally ill that commit horrible crimes, but 'sane' people also commit horrifying crimes. What this politician doesn't realize is that the majority of the mentally ill are just trying to gasp for air. He is nothing more than a power hungry selfish fuck who should keep his mouth shut.*

*As I am lying on the couch I feel a strong desire to go back to Table Mountain. I get up and go. The sun is still out and it is hot but I can see the sun starting to vanish on the horizon. There are no clouds or sunset that inspires Grace falling down. I look at my feet and wonder if I have done enough damage to my body. I take off my shoes and start walking bare foot. I parked two blocks away from the trail head. I am listening to music that makes me think of walking on coals. Some people would say that I am crazy, well, I realize that and have known that for a long time, so fuck'em. I have a book with me about world religions and am reading it as I walk. I don't know why I get so hung up on religious stuff but I am looking for a bit of truth. I make my way to the top of the mountain and I read. I just wonder why religions can't co-exist.*

*It is dark now and my water bottle is empty. The water I drank has given me new life. I have a fire in my belly and I am pissed at everyone. Fuck everyone. I get on the side of the mountain and start running on the trail again. My feet are throbbing. I need to feel alive for a moment. I can see outside of myself and there are all these energies. Do I look like a warrior or do I look like a madman?*

*I then decide to ask the world (or God) a simple question. The street lights are glimmering below and house lights are on but I can't see their lights. I can't believe how many people don't know about mental illness and don't care. The politician and his ignorance inspire a rage that boils my blood. I look out at the lights and I just want to breathe them all in and the judgments made of me. I want to breathe fire out and judge everyone for their blindness.*

# 35
## Color Wheel

*It has been a month and the delusions and voices are still with me. I can feel the Seroquel pumping through my veins and it makes me mild like trees with no leaves. I have a dream of Diana standing tall with little cabinets all around her. It is dark.*

*I hear the gypsy's voice and I tell her at this point I don't want to have anything to do with her. What can I do to get her out of my head? I can't control the voices and her voice speaks to me that one day we will find each other in this mess. I don't want her and I don't want life anymore.*

*I decide to go for a walk on the forestry trail. I am listening to music and there is a spot that talks about marking your territory in the song. I picture myself holding a staff and hitting it to the ground. As I hit the ground a rainbow of colors spreads everywhere. I finally see the colors. It makes me feel like we can share the land with one another.*

*I keep walking and end up at the park where a car that has been taken apart is and I look at all the pieces. Someone must have littered them there. I am going to head home. I spend the day lost in my confusion. It is the afternoon and I decide to go out again. I am riding my bike on the long trail and there are rabbits everywhere. All of a sudden I see a large circular fabric lying on the ground. The inside is rainbow colors and it sort of freaks me out because of the vision I had with the staff hitting the ground and watching the colors spread. Is God still trying to say something to me? I have relinquished control and go with the flow. Wherever he leads, I follow. What should I think of this coincidence? I find myself home, watching TV. There is a show about hot air balloons and the balloon has rainbow colors. Is all of this color stuff a coincidence or is God talking to me and letting me know that I still have a chance to give back. What are the odds of someone leaving that on the trail? What are the odds of seeing it on a hot air balloon?*

*I am taking a different walk today. I decide to walk on the street for a change. I walk past a high school and sit and meditate in the middle of the football field. There are only a few people there and I relax and try to focus on nothing. I decide to walk home and a group of guys drive by and start screaming at me. They flip me off and I just want to know what their problem is. I raise my hand and the car turns around and comes back toward me. Before I know it I have four guys with crystal meth coating their stained bodies standing in front of me. They start to push me and I am in no mood to squabble with four meth heads. The look on one guy's face is terrifying. His brow has "no mercy" written on it and I can see that he is ready to bury me for no reason. I want to know what their problem is but they are in no mood to tell me. I suppose there is a reason and I must reflect something in their hearts that calls for a beating. I can't understand why someone would fight for no reason. I back off and put my head down and avoid the beating by acting humble. I make my way home humiliated but glad that I'm not spitting blood. I remember so long ago when I wanted a beating to reflect redemption but there are no signs of that anymore.*

*There is an apartment when I walk through the streets that has a huge cement pole on it. I notice it when I walk the streets. The same day I met with the crystal meth guys is the same day that I see that someone has bulldozed it over. Someone must have smashed* into it. I wondered who could do this. The next day I saw a tree after we had a bad wind storm that was uprooted. I couldn't figure out how such a huge tree could be uprooted like that and there was a coincidence of seeing two mighty things broken. There is so much damage in the last few days I wondered if I am headed toward the same random destruction. I am ready for it. I am so tired of hearing these voices and feeling desperate that I want it to end.

The days keep tumbling.

I hope I can find myself again. The energy is outside of me and I can't control it. My mind is spinning. Will I be me again?

Muttle
Muttle
Muttle


I love Bob Marley and I know he was a huge soccer player so I picture us in the backyard playing together. There are ten or twelve trees in a line. I kick the soccer ball between two trees and I keep doing that down the line. I kick and think the United States should stop fighting everybody. The war on terror is as futile as the war on drugs. There will always be terror because the U.S. invades these countries and kills people there. I wonder what it would be like if we stopped invading these territories and invested in peace keepers. Maybe we could have fifty, a hundred, a thousand, ten thousand, a hundred thousand people come into the country and raise up schools and show how to be economically practical. If we bombarded them with peace and goodwill they could look at our country as something positive and truly change the lives of the terrorists. They should help build up civilizations instead of tearing them down. I kick the ball through the trees and think of all the countries that would prosper. I kick through one country and then I kick it through another. I do this with every country I can think of.

I also think of genocide and how we would finally get a chance to use our weapons of madness for something good. This soccer game goes on for a while.

I have the poison and the meds in me. They make me

*uneducated. I can't think through these ideas. If only the voices would stop. I can live with the signs and omens but the voices are getting unbearable.*

*The days roll.*

*I ride my bike and I walk. The hopeless man trying to grip reality is me. If I didn't have my family I would be a walking madmen, homeless and without hope. I wonder how the mentally ill people on the streets do it. I also wonder how the mentally ill in prison can handle being locked up in a tiny cell. If that were me I would truly lose my mind. I come home to smiling faces: my mom, my sister and little Jayde, and I know that I am loved and have love to give.*

*I have a bunch of shoes. I walk around trying to imagine what it would be like to be in a different culture. I think of all the calloused people in the world and realize that their hearts aren't like mine. We build these icons and think they are unique but we forget that all you have to do is walk outside and speak to someone and find joy in it.*

*Time keeps moving slowly and another strange thing happens to me. When I go walking up the trail there is a house where the backyard is facing the trail. On this day I am not listening to music. I hear a child lightly singing a song. She is about seven. She stops singing and looks at me. She says, "I believe in you, I believe in you, I believe in you." This startles me. It fucking freaks me out. She believes in me for what? I am no savior. I have sickness in me. Maybe God shows me signs for a reason. Maybe there is potential in me and something worth believing in. After she speaks the words she starts singing softly again. Why does she believe in me? What does she want me to do? Through the mouths of babes: I can't be your savior. I am no Messiah, I am no False Prophet. I am just keeping my feet on the ground waiting and listening to God's whispers. I have grown tired of trying to carry the world on my shoulders. Maybe someday God will put me in the place I belong with the right people to commune with.*

It has been a few months since the little girl said she believed in me. As I take my usual walk, I listen to depressing music. There is something comforting about it.

Today is a special day -- as I walk from the park, suddenly, the energy and delusions and scrambled thoughts flow out of my head.

I am me again.

It happened.

It finally happened.

I fell to my knees and put my head on the pavement.

I am finally me again. I am finally me. I can feel it!

I found myself again! The voices are gone! The voices are gone! I am finally me!

The days after my transformation were so nice. It had happened and I was so thankful for my second chance. I finally realized that I would need the medicine for the rest of my life. It is hard to get that idea through a thick skull but I was tired. The high's with bipolar are similar to cocaine. The ups are so intense and they can be exciting to feel, but I had to stop chasing the highs and keep my peace of mind. I thought I would find heaven in a maze, but realize that I could be complete with a bland gaze.

Because of this life-changing event I decide I have to keep one foot in front of the other and learn to trust love.

I went back to work at the coffee shop.

A new girl was in my life and her name was Jenny. We met over the internet in a chat room. She and I spend many nights just talking on the phone. We have the same taste in music and she burns CDs for me of new bands that she likes. She has sort of an 'emo' side to her, but I listen to the music and give it a chance. My roots are still strong listening to all kinds of different music and I am always keeping my ears open. She is super cute and has a fresh outlook on life. I am so damaged and it is good to be with someone as fresh and unique as a sunflower. She is a couple of years younger than me and we have fun together.

My delusions aren't strong anymore but they somehow are still with me and I sometimes see signs the way I used to. Maybe after a couple of months they will all be gone. The first night Jenny and I met, she drove thirty minutes to see me. Her car was a stick shift and she didn't know how to drive it. I gave her an hour long lesson. She worked in a coffee shop so we had that in common. It was again nice to be with someone other than a gypsy vibrating in my mind. To be with flesh was so kind. We dated for a while but eventually I think we got bored with each other. I think I was just lonely and that was why we were dating so I stopped seeing her.

I was back at work and having trouble working as a mule again with meds that were pulsing in my body and brain. I was sleeping 16 hours a day and it was almost impossible to wake up early and go to the coffee shop for work. The leave of absence was nice but how could I carry on like this. I kept punching the clock but forgetting how I got through the days. My friend Millie was the shift supervisor and she was on me like crazy. I couldn't explain to her that it was the meds and when I did she still expected me to be at par or above. I didn't blame her. When someone can't do a job they shouldn't be there. I tried so hard to work hard but I just didn't have it in me. I eventually got fired for showing up one hour late. I could have fought it and gotten my job back because of my disability but I was too ashamed of letting people know my weakness.

# 36

## The Flight

Six months after getting fired, I felt like the old me; the same guy that used to go out with Kelly, Millie and Dustin and head to the Rio for the strongest margaritas in the world. I was still affected by the meds, but not as much.

I was playing music on stage at the Blue Canyon and when I started to change from one harmonica to the other, I grabbed the metal bracing and my hand started shaking. I couldn't open the harmonica contraption to put the harmonica in. My hand was shaking because of the lithium. I finally pressed it against my leg, which worked.

It was New Year's Eve, which was a special night for me. I always loved New Year's Eve because it seemed like the one night when everyone was happy. I was meeting with some coffee shop friends downtown and I thought I would take the light rail so I didn't have to drive in the madness.

On my way to the light rail, I stopped and bought a bottle of Jim Beam. I love whisky, but it does not love me. It is the one drink that always makes me sick. I think because I like it so much and I just keep drinking it. I know I shouldn't drink on my meds, but, hey, I was thinking straight now and one night wasn't going to kill me. I felt I needed to dabble in a little booze now and then. I realized I would have to drive home drunk from the light rail station but that shouldn't be an issue. I was sure Millie would let me crash at her place. I opened a can of cola and drank half of it on my way to the light rail. I then took my bottle of Jim Beam and poured it in the can. I bought a big bottle because I figured I could just sip on it all night and not have to pay so much for drinks.

I was dressed in black. I never dressed up any more but I had all my suits from the loan officer job. I was wearing a black leather strap around my neck but it fit with the black suit, shirt, socks and shoes. After I was dressed up and looking at myself in the mirror, I thought of Johnny Cash and his song, "The Man in Black." It just felt right to dress in black. I looked like a swanky business prick, but I felt like an old 50's rockabilly guy. It is funny sometimes how you see yourself compared to how others see you.

I made my way to the light rail stop and stood next to a goofy-looking cop. He immediately said, "So, do you have some booze in that can?"

I looked at him and said, "Absolutely. I also have some crystal meth in my shoes." He started laughing. It is amazing how easy it is to bullshit if you're not out of your mind with delusions.

He and I sat and talked and he told me about some guy he just busted that had alcohol in his pop can. The cop said, "Man, he looked so guilty."

Somewhere along the line, I learned how to con a cop.

The light rail arrived and I stepped on. I looked back at the cop and saw a man desperately holding on to a principle. The light rail was fast and there was graffiti along the way. I love that particular kind of art. It reminds me of London and the graffiti on the walls for the passengers on the trains to admire. There is so much of it in London. I have seen so much and have changed like water into ice. I was someone who could look in the mirror and smile. I was the old me and I wasn't looking for a place to fit in. I fit in my own shoes just fine.

There were many different people on the train. Mostly 21 year olds ready to party. I kept to myself and sipped quietly on my can. I didn't feel like chatting with anyone. There wasn't much to do on the train but look out the window at the cars and people. I've always been the daydreamer who sits and ponders and watches.

The light rail stopped at Union Station and the first thing I did after stepping off the light rail was stick a cigarette in my mouth. I was smoking again. I then threw the empty bottle in the trash and laughed at the fact that I drank it so fast. I also laughed because I had a nice buzz. I started walking toward the Paramount where I was going to meet everyone. It was quite a walk and there were many people in downtown Denver.

As I walked along, I saw a homeless guy. I put my head down and kept walking. I thought of the gentle street walker with his lizard looking hands. Then I thought of another incident I had with a homeless guy: We were downtown, walking from the bar Fado's to the Jazz Bar up the street. This homeless guy was playing his guitar outside a bar that we were passing. That poor guy sounded bad. His voice was off key and his guitar was not tuned. I didn't put any change in his hat. Instead, I looked the homeless guy in the eye and gave him a nod. I then stopped to listen to his music. A rich, young, blond, white man, with a slick buttoned down shirt and black pants came by and stood next to the homeless guy. I heard the blond guy say in the most condescending way, "You are so terrific at the guitar and your voice is amazing. I bet you will get a record contract soon, I just can't believe how good you are. FREAK." The homeless guy's head fell. I did nothing to defend him, which was shameful. My friend Dustin knew I was going to kick the shit out of the blond guy and held me back.

Tonight is different. Everyone is fun on New Year's Eve, so I looked forward to seeing smiling faces from my friends. For the next three blocks I thought about how hard the streets can be. I kept moving on as these memories trickled in my mind.

The Paramount is next to the 410 building I worked in when I was "a business man." I finally arrived and I saw my friend Tami. Tami had dated Alex and Alex told her that she was not allowed to speak to me (must have been jealousy). She and I have become close since they broke up. She works at the coffee shop. I saw Millie and Cori and then I saw one of Millie's friends. The girl was pretty; not too pretty, but in my book, pretty. I said hello to everyone. Tami came over and plopped down next to me and told me that if she didn't find a guy to make out with then she was making out with me. We all laughed.

I worked my charms on the blonde girl (Millie's friend). She was not easily charmed. She told me that she had just gotten out of a bad relationship. I was so drunk that I didn't care and I most certainly didn't want to hear all about it, so I moved on.

The drinks kept flowing and we were doing tons of shots. I thought back about the eight ounces of whisky I drank earlier and realized that was why I was so hammered. I couldn't believe how drunk I was.

I ended up alone, which was cool by me. I was usually alone. The blonde girl told me that she might hook up with an older guy. I didn't care. I would tap-dance in hardware stores and try to do Charlie Chaplin impersonations in the street, but I figured I was not going to let some frizzy headed blonde waste my time. There was so much energy. I was pumped with so much Lithium, Seroquel, Clonazepam and alcohol that I finally felt alive. I normally didn't drink like this but I was tired of the blandness and how it was stirring in my veins.

The night moved on and Tami and Cori had decided to go home with two guys. Well, Tami could do whatever she wanted but Cori was an innocent little Christian girl. I immediately disapproved and told both of them in front of their guys that they shouldn't go home with random guys. I was mostly thinking of Cori because I knew her family from the coffee shop and I wanted to protect her. The girls made it clear that they were going home with these guys and the guys made it clear that they were taking them home. It pissed me off but what could I do.

When it was time to leave, I had probably had about fifteen drinks. I never drank that much anymore, but maybe I was just depressed. I had to piss. I walked through the bar and made my way upstairs to the restrooms. I had to pee. As I was standing in the stall, which was packed with guys, I overheard a guy say to his friend: "So are you going to fuck her tonight?" Now this made me mad because of what had just happened downstairs and I felt surrounded by self-serving, selfish pricks. I tried to pee and I couldn't. I was mad and I couldn't relax enough to piss. I stood there and listened to more.

"She looks like she will put out. Definitely."

"She is going to be so easy."

"She will beg me for more when I'm finished with her."

Laugh, laugh, laugh.

I was out of there. I felt sick. I guess everyone has sex with random strangers but that was not how I operated. I like to know someone first, but I guess I am old-fashioned. I made my way down the stairs and pushed my way to the table. We then all pushed our way outside and across the street.

By this time I had to piss so bad that I couldn't stand it. I walked down Sixteenth Street. I had to piss so I finally found the perfect jewelry store with shiny drops of glob hanging from the wall. I thought it would be fitting for me to piss by this symbol of wealth. It is strange that a guy can't piss in a confined, designated area but can piss while a crowd of hundreds pass by him. I was drunk but even as drunk as I was, this drunkenness did not compare to my mellowest bipolar moment. This was one on a scale of ten, with ten being bipolar, dancing with fire. So, I let it flow and I felt more at home not caring about the crowds than I did in the confines of layered stalls.

As I was standing there pissing I heard a big hairy guy say, "You're a fucking freak." (He definitely used the wrong word!) I realized that he had no clue what I had been through. I thought of the word freak and remembered the homeless guy who was called a freak way back by the bar. He was with me now, with me like a two hands clasping.

That word reminded me of all the people who had been accused of being "that word." In the mental hospital I made friends with these lonely souls that will never fit in anywhere and the people that have no one to look out for them. He didn't know that I almost drowned in the quicksand and pulled myself out of it. I stood there and thought about the people that see machines; and my anger was so strong that I couldn't contain it. I was shaking from the lithium but the booze was keeping me steady.

There is a point when a man knows he is going to fight. He can smell it. It's adrenaline. I knew what I was going to do. I also knew that there were seven of them and I was going to probably get the crap kicked out of me. Why not? It was time to go. I decided to start with big mouth first. The anger was building. I was crossing the line. I was taking an ambush stride. The muscles in my legs were burning and the desire to beat the fuck out of these guys was so strong that I surprised myself. I'm a passive person but it was time to take action. It was time for me to fight for the homeless guy. I could see the seven of them all gathered and the last thing I thought about before I plowed into them was both my Grandpa Tolini and my brother. They were the boxers. I wasn't a boxer but I was fighting for this. I thought about making my strikes sharp.

None of these guys knew what was coming and as I started swinging my anger completely took over. I threw all my weight into it and watched the hairy, mouthy man fall forward. He hit the ground before he could open his mouth to say 'the word' again. This was just the beginning. (Honestly, I can't remember what happened. I sort of blacked out.) I remember rambling around with a bunch of them. I also remember trying to get away and one of "mouth's" friends tackling me and pushing me but I didn't fall down. I hunched over and I looked back at him. His was close enough for a good elbow. My elbow flew out and hit him in the jaw. At this point I was trying to get away from them. I had made my presence known and it was time to get the fuck out of there. The elbow was not an angry hit but more of a survival hit. I then slipped into the huge crowd like a ghost.

They didn't see me as I melted into the crowd and I walked down Sixteenth Street looking for Millie. When I saw her, she asked me where I had been and I said, "I was just fighting." She looked away in disgust. She didn't give me the opportunity to tell her about the justice I had fought for. She just looked away in disgust.

What I did was wrong. I could have hurt the guy and I have to live with that. But someone has to stand up and say, "Fuck it!" when some arrogant asshole abuses the weak, and tonight was that night for me. I was the weak. Anyone who has ever been called a freak is the weak. However, fighting solves nothing and it doesn't change people. Alcohol drove me. Alcohol took my anger and reason and took control. I don't know if I want to drink to that point again, where you lose all control. I would rather be with my friends and have enough to give me a buzz and keep my thoughts clear. I shouldn't be drinking alcohol with the meds I take anyway. I'm trying to stop but when your friends' culture is to drink, it takes a strong man to still hang out and not have any.

The cab ride home to Millie's on New Year's Eve was quiet. I figured that Millie and the blonde couldn't understand why I fought so I didn't even try to justify it to them.

You can tell stories about mental delusions and hallucinations and people might listen, but to truly understand you have to live and breathe it. Life gives us all secrets that make you want to curl up in the corner and never step out to the middle of the room. I felt like I had curled up in the corner for too long and I needed to let go of my prison.

In the morning Millie took me to my car and I drove home. I thought about who I was and where I wanted to go. I will always be passionate for people, and hopefully I will always want to defend and support the poor hopeless men and women who suffer mental illness. Most of them have no one who will listen to them, much less support them.

The next day I felt pride. Pride in standing up, pride in growing up. I put my headphones on and went for the usual walk. We were the so called 'freaks.' I remember my brother telling me about my potential and how I had to follow my gut. I acted instead of talking. I acted.

Three months have passed and I have barely had any alcohol. It's hard to not drink with my friends but my friends and I have gotten used to my sobriety. They understand and support me. Self medication could lead me back to the hospital. So will I self medicate or will I not? Will I stop taking my meds again because the highs were so high? -- Only time will tell.

# Final Chapter

I walk to the junked car in the field by my house. The walk is nice and a slim callous voice is ringing in my ear. Not quite like the old days but I feel the music. I sit down in a comfortable spot. I wonder if I will ever live up to the goals I set now for myself. Yeah, I'm not crazy anymore, but those days are with me like burning coal. They always will be and although I sit and try to describe a bi-polar schizoaffective person, I know that you have to live it to truly understand. I guess I realize how thankful I am for getting a second chance. So many mentally ill people walk around looking for their piece of gold in a haze and will never find it while the machines bark at them and hold them in their place. It is a hard thing to give yourself over to the meds. But they have saved me and my mind and I wish for that with all people that are mentally ill. It's hard to give up the delusion but it is the road so many sick people need to make.

I still want to make my millions of dollars. I want to start a non-profit company that gives more than ten percent back to help, to change, to affect. Abundance for myself follows screaming behind.

How will I get there? I know things don't come easy and you have to work hard for what you have. My grandpa worked so hard. It is time to work. What should I do? Try to make it in music? Not likely. Should I write a book? Should I work on my art? Well, graphic designers don't make anything and neither does an average charcoal artist. I realize that following the passion of art is going to be a hobby after I have made something I am truly proud to be. The real world is finally coming into view and I am okay with it. I think I have known for a long time that I might end up doing a job that I am not completely enthralled with, so I will always "mop the floors."

I wonder if someday the poor men in the US will walk on avenues of bureaucrats, stomping on all of them. I wonder if one day an average man will not be a slave. I guess I am a slave, a slave in my walls. But life is also delicious. Life is a mess of sipping dreams and solid streams. A slave sometimes lives like a king and sometimes a king lives like a slave.

Maybe I'll join the peace corp. That would be a way to affect people. I could just see me in some random country working hard to build tiny block houses. Maybe I will just be average, have a little wife, a little car, a little house, with little kids. I like that idea.

It seems everyone is trying to be special with voices that ring.

There is hope for a madman. A freak in the past has been my name but there is hope to turn madness into control. There is hope for families that feel despair for someone in their family that has a mental illness. There is hope for the people with mental illness in a drugged up state of consciousness to function in our world. I will stand up for the weak no matter what I do. I will stand when the drugs pulsing through me tell me to sit the fuck down. I will fight it like rushing upstream when the water is choking. I will stand, and if I hear the word "freak," the gloves on my hands might fire off tiny explosions again. Someone has to say, "Stop." Someone has to. This can stop if we let go of rage and make change.

And as far as "truth" mentioned in the beginning chapter, life is a moment of truth in a reality of infinite small pieces that feels like ticking clocks with each picture showing its face. That is just a simple-minded man's opinion. We are all ticking to our own clocks and the future could be pillars of small lights which become absolute lights with absolute truths shining on everything.

Just dreams.

# Acknowledgments

*Thank you to my family for all their support even when I was as low as I was. I want to thank Dinah Tolini, Bethany Wolf and Mark Sharp for their guidance in editing the book. I would also like to thank Cherish Solutions for their help with graphic design and layout.*

## Tobyn's Music

Tobyn is also the creator of 2 CDs. The first one is called "STUMBLING DOWN" and the second one is called " THE LONG WAY AROUND". You can hear the music on iTunes, Amazonmp3 and dozens of other distribution channels.

18185031R00158

Made in the USA
San Bernardino, CA
02 January 2015